Alternative Strings

The New Curriculum

Alternative Strings

The New Curriculum

Julie Lyonn Lieberman

AMADEUS PRESS, LLC
Pompton Plains ✦ Cambridge

Published in 2004 by

Amadeus Press, LLC
512 Newark Pompton Turnpike
Pompton Plains, New Jersey 07444
U.S.A.

Amadeus Press
2 Station Road
Swavesey
Cambridge CB4 5QJ, U.K.

For sales, please contact

NORTH AMERICA

AMADEUS PRESS, LLC
c/o Hal Leonard Corp.
7777 West Bluemound Road
Milwaukee, Wisconsin 53213 U.S.A.
Tel. 800-637-2852
Fax 414-774-3259

UNITED KINGDOM AND EUROPE

AMADEUS PRESS
2 Station Road
Swavesey, Cambridge, CB4 5QJ, U.K.
Tel. 01954-232959
Fax 01954-206040

E-mail: orders@amadeuspress.com
Website: www.amadeuspress.com

Design and production by Snow Creative Services
Printed in the United States of America

Library of Congress Cataloging-in-Publication Data

Lieberman, Julie Lyonn.
  Alternative strings : the new curriculum / Julie Lyonn Lieberman.—
  Original paperback ed.
      p. cm.
Includes discographies and index.
  ISBN 1-57467-089-1
  1. Stringed instruments—Instruction and study. 2. Violin—Instruction and study. 3. Stringed instruments—Performance. I. Title.
MT259.L54 2004
787'.193—dc22

2003021359

Contents

Table of Contents: Audio CD

Words of wisdom from alternative string performers and clinicians:

*   Used with permission: WEMP Milwaukee Broadcast April 16, 1940

** Excerpt of ASTA 2003 clinic, recorded live

*** Used with permission: Huiksi Music (piano, Armen Donelian; bass, Jeffry Eckels; drums, Steve Johns)

CD engineered by Paul Jacobs

Acknowledgments

Special thanks to John Cerullo and Carol Flannery at Amadeus Press, to my fabulous editor Joanna Dalin, and to my incredible graphic designer Michael Snow for each playing a major role in the successful creation of this work.

The embroidered violin on the cover was created by Chun "Robin" Elkins and inspired by Curt Childress. Linda Kuruc provided me with the photograph of a beach in Nova Scotia. Without knowing one another, all three co-created the cover through Michael Snow. Many thanks to each of them.

I would also like to thank all of the wonderful friends, students, and colleagues who helped me maneuver the final details of the book and helped create the audio CD:

Matt Fichtenbaum, Margie Baron, Jennifer Axelson, Bill Caspary, Vicki Horner Richards, Greg Harbar, Howard Armstrong, Geoffrey Fitzhugh Perry, Martha Mooke, Ed Caner, Daryl Silberman, Mark Wood, Anthony Barnett, Jesus Florido, Randy Sabien, Leanne Darling, Bob Phillips, Julianna Waller, Martin Norgaard, Richard Greene, and Claude Williams. Thanks also go to Tom Carruth of Coda Music and engineer Paul Jacobs for help on the technical side.

Preface

Growing numbers of string teachers are integrating alternative strings into their curriculum. I thought it would be far better for you to learn about the effects of this inclusive approach to string education from some actual students. Here are the opinions of twenty-five young string players from different areas of the country:

"Learning fiddling styles has made a big difference in my playing. Because I am playing with friends, I have a much higher confidence level. I am more active in my regular orchestra class and have more incentive to practice. I have grown closer to my friends and I look forward to our wonderful fiddle club each week."

Kathlyn Carroll, junior
Duluth High School, Georgia

"Fiddling has opened my view of what viola music is a lot! I thought I would have to play the guitar to play anything other than classical music. Now I play all kinds of music on my viola! Many more kinds of music than I ever knew about!"

Christine Hedden, seventh grader
Dodd Middle School, Cheshire, Connecticut

"Playing alternative music on my violin has made me enthusiastic about playing again. While I will always play classical music, being able to play non-classical styles brings exciting new energy to my playing. I love it!"

Judy Evans, adult student
Concord, California

"It rocks! You can make up your own song and, no matter what you play, it can't be wrong!"

Alden Wheeler, sixth grader
Atchison County Community Middle School, Effingham, Kansas

"Improvisation is lots of fun. It is quite different for me, because I am used to reading music in my orchestra. I can improvise for hours and love it! I sometimes wish that I could remember better some of the fun melodies that I have created. It is very cool to feel free and be able to express my music without being bound to the notes on the page."

Austin Childress, seventh grader
Frontier Trail Middle School, Olathe, Kansas

"As a freshman, when I heard about fiddling in the fiddle club I was very interested. The skills I've learned while playing in the fiddle club have taken me from last chair in the freshman orchestra to concertmaster of our middle orchestra in my junior year."

Audrey Lee, junior
Duluth High School, Georgia

"When I first began fiddle club, I expected to learn the tunes with sheet music, but that wasn't right at all! It was hard to learn the first few pieces by ear. I really got into adding modifications and that made me stick with it. Now learning tunes by ear is easier and I have learned a lot more ways to vary the tunes, too. I am having a lot of fun with this and I am really glad that I am learning to fiddle."

Justin Ivey, eighth grader
Dodd Middle School, Cheshire, Connecticut

"Fiddling has been a great opportunity for me. I like fiddling because you learn to play fast and it is cool and the tunes are so different! You learn so much and it is fun while you do it. It is so much fun that sometimes practicing my fiddle tunes and techniques helps take my mind off my everyday work."

Mary O'Donnell, seventh grader
St. Catherine of Siena, Trumbull, Connecticut

"Fiddling is more fun for me than classical music because it is less formal, and there are less rules and more freedom to put myself into the music. I like learning all the different styles of fiddling, too. I enjoy myself, my instrument, and performing more when I am fiddling."

Josh Liebskind, eighth grader
Dodd Middle School, Cheshire, Connecticut

"I'll never forget seeing my parents looking up at me as they danced to my solo on the Ash Grove waltz at our barn dance last spring. I like being able to play the melody my way and I like getting to write my own bass lines, too!"

William Si, eighth grader
Dodd Middle School, Cheshire, Connecticut

"I've been playing violin for about six years, and in that time fiddling has let me express myself the most. Playing fiddle styles really doesn't have any rules...you can do anything. And 'wrong' notes aren't always wrong. Fiddling has taught me a lot about expression while playing. If you play because that's the note... then bah! You have to feel the music yourself before your audience can. By learning to play by ear on the violin, I've been able to play by ear on the guitar and piano. When I'm having a really bad day, I can listen to or play some music, classical or fiddle, and it makes me feel a bit better.... If you can master the fiddle you can play ANYTHING!"

Piper Benjamin, junior
Duluth High School, Georgia

"Through playing fiddle music, I have been inspired to learn as much about music from different cultures of the world as I can. I have learned a sense of style that I didn't have before. Mostly, it has improved the way I think about music."

Sylvia Hartley, junior
Duluth High School, Georgia

"Learning to improvise has helped me become a more developed player on my instrument by improving my listening skills in my orchestra class. Even though I have been playing music for years, there is always room to learn more techniques and new styles of playing."

Megan Hernandez, junior
Duluth High School, Georgia

"Improvisation is so Cool! I like doing improvisation because there are no sour notes! You feel free, and you don't mess up when you don't have any notes to follow. You can do it whenever or wherever you are because all you need is your violin and the accompaniment music. I just play and play and play because I love it!"

Kymmee Noll, third grader
Jefferson County North Elementary School, Nortonville, Kansas

"If music is the speech of angels, then fiddling is...well, we'll have to think about that one. But in honesty, the use of new techniques and styles not only encourages appreciation of the diversity of music, but also introduces a whole new idea of music—what it is and can become. Learning improvisation, experimenting, and even making mistakes all can be another music class altogether, but I think that being able to use all of it in any situation helps to discover the potential a musician can achieve or at least try to achieve. So maybe it's speech therapy."

Annie Pullagra, sophomore
Duluth High School, Georgia

"Fiddling has helped me express my opinions more openly and loudly. It has also helped with vibrato. Another thing is improved tuning [intonation] because we use our ears to learn the songs so we memorize the sounds."

Timothy Leviton, junior
Duluth High School, Georgia

"Playing different styles has really changed my attitude about music. Sometimes when I play a classical piece, I think about how I could convert it to a different style. It opens my mind to new possibilities."

Zoë Atlas, sixth grader
Albany Middle School, California

"Improvising using the notes of the D scale is fun! It gives you something to call your own."

Sloan Elias, sixth grader
Atchison County Community Middle School, Effingham, Kansas

"Improvising with the D scale is awesome! You can do anything with it and it still sounds awesome!"

Jennifer Harmon, sixth grader
Atchison County Community Middle School, Effingham, Kansas

"I like playing all the fast notes and playing drones so that I can play more than one string at once! If you enjoy being creative when you play, fiddling is for you!"

Shichu Jing, seventh grader
Dodd Middle School, Cheshire, Connecticut

"Fiddling actually helps you improve your playing and helps you understand about chords and the structure of the tunes you learn. I love that everyone can be playing their own variations at the same time—and it sounds even better together!"

Amy Xie, freshman
James H. Moran Middle School, Wallingford, Connecticut

"I like fiddling because the tunes are short enough for you to learn by ear and you can add things like your own bowings and extra notes. It is a whole different way to play the violin than classical music!"

Jenny Gi, seventh grader
Dodd Middle School, Cheshire, Connecticut

"What I've always enjoyed about fiddle music is the endless variety. You never hear a tune played the same way twice."

David Delaney, homeschooler
South Windsor, Connecticut

"Improvisation has helped me breathe life into my music. Not to mention that jamming out at the drop of a hat impresses the relatives. Fiddling has given me a larger repertoire of music to play around with and it's way more fun than just playing by the notes."

Jennifer Barnett, senior
Duluth High School, Georgia

Introduction

1

I had the great fortune to grow up in a family that introduced me to a wide panorama of styles. My grandparents took me to the opera and the Tanglewood Music Festival, and my parents were just as likely to spin Benny Goodman, Pete Seeger, Leadbelly, or Paul Robeson on the turntable as Bach. Because my family played an important role in forming the Folk Music Society of Northern New Jersey, I enjoyed constant exposure to blues and world music, as well as to American vernacular music and, like everyone else my age, I had recordings by the Beatles and other popular groups of the time. I took this richly diverse exposure for granted until I reached college and encountered the classical emphasis prevalent among many—if not most—college music departments. The other string players my age had only experienced the straight and narrow: classical and more classical.

Julie Lyonn Lieberman

photo by Randall Wallace

There were never any conflicts between my diverse musical interests. I grew up studying classical violin with Samuel Applebaum, Nancy Clarke, Stanley Ritchie, and William Henry. I also attended Manhattan School of Music Prep Division, where I studied with Romuald Tecco. He had just arrived from training with Galamian in Europe. I experienced everything I practiced as music, not as specific styles. I enjoyed my classical studies as much as the fiddle tunes I was learning from Dave Richardson of the Boys of the Lough and the swing and blues tunes I was performing with David Amram, Papa John Kolstad, Lewis London, and other artists active on the folk music scene.

I dropped out of high school orchestra in my sophomore year. I feel certain that I, like many other string players, would have remained in the orchestra had the music included folk, jazz, and popular styles. I know that I wasn't the only string player who longed for greater diversity. Thinking back on who I was at that time, I am sure that I wasn't particularly articulate about my feelings. Like so many other young players, I lost interest and left. Now, decades later, as I tour the country working with string classes and orchestras, I recognize on the faces of the students the same look I must have had on my face: one that reflects disconnection, disinterest, and disengagement. I have also had the pleasure of seeing those same faces beam with curiosity and excitement as we have explored styles that are new to them or played games designed to engage their creative playfulness.

By my sophomore year in college, I began to wake up to the fact that I was being treated differently, that I didn't fit in. The more deeply I became involved with alternative styles and composition in those styles, the more the music faculty at Sarah Lawrence College snubbed me. I had started studying jazz off-campus with Sal Mosca, protégé of Lennie Tristano. I remember telling my violin teacher, Bill Henry, co-founder of the Orpheus Ensemble and my only ally, that I felt something else beckoning to me musically but had no idea what it was. He always expressed certainty that I would figure it out. That meant a great deal to me at the time because I felt entirely lost. Only Bill came to my senior recital (he flew in from a concert tour in Europe), comprised of Bartók, original compositions, and a few fiddle and jazz tunes. Some faculty even insulted me after I graduated by snubbing a few students who opted to study privately with me off campus. I have long since released any resentment. I now understand that those educators were only doing what had been done to them: trying to teach me to wear the harness and wear it well.

While my history may be of little interest on its own, I share it as representative of issues we still face today. Do we realize how many students have an appetite for styles outside the classical curriculum? Are we willing to open up traditional teaching practices to embrace the musical imagination of the world? Why can't the learning experience—from the middle school classroom to the conservatory—offer a process of exploration, discovery, creativity, and joyfulness while making music?

Over the last thirty years, through teaching private lessons and workshops nationwide, I've been privy to the emotional lives of thousands of classical string players. I have yet to meet anyone shaped by the rigors of classical training who had a "happy childhood," musically speaking. Why has that been, and is it an acceptable experience worth perpetuating? To raise a fine, deep-thinking next generation, don't we need to cultivate original thinking? Can we learn to trust the fact that if we expose students to all genres, then each, including classical, will thrive? I think so.

Today, the sheer number of materials available to would-be fiddlers or jazzers has multiplied so rapidly that the alternative string community simply cannot be ignored.

My intention in writing this book is to provide you with a resource that will help you stay up-to-date both as a player and as an educator, and to encourage you to honor and include all musical traditions as well as the art of improvisation.

Alternative Strings

2

W hat Do We Mean by "Alternative"?

At present, *alternative* is the catch phrase for close to thirty folk, world, jazz, and popular styles that feature strings, including:

American Folk (5)	World (15)
Bluegrass	Afro-Cuban
Cajun	Arabic
Franco-American	Bossa Nova
Old-Time	Cape Breton
Western Swing	East Indian (Carnatic and Hindustani)
	Flamenco
Jazz (4)	Greek
Bebop	Gypsy
Blues	Irish
Modern	Klezmer
Swing	Mexican (Tierra Caliente and Mariachi)
	Scandinavian (Swedish, Norwegian,
Contemporary (3)	Danish, and Finnish)
Hip Hop	Scottish
Pop Music	Shetland Island
Rock	Tango

The surge in diverse string activity has engendered a hunt within the string community for accurate descriptors. We simply have not known what to call ourselves. At first, of course, it was easy:

photo by Anne Hamersky

Darol Anger

"I'm an Irish fiddler," "I'm a jazz violinist," "I'm a blues fiddler," and so on. But many string players have branched out to encompass more than one style, so we have had to develop new descriptions. For instance, Turtle Island String Quartet co-founder Darol Anger called himself an "American vernacular fiddler" until he changed his title to "freestyle fiddler." For some, the term *jazz violinist* shifted to *improvising violinist*. *Multi-style fiddler* and *fusion violinist* have floated around as well.

Recently, the American String Teacher Association (ASTA) realized that this expansive movement within the string community should be recognized. The organization decided to embrace and include non-classical styles in its identity. The small committee for the 2003 ASTA conference "All Together Now," made up of Andy Dabcynzski, Matt Glaser, Renata Bratt, Dr. Stanley Chepaitis, Robert Gardner, and myself, struggled during its first few conference calls in search of what to call this movement. The term *non-classical* implied that classical was innately superior, so we discarded that title. In the end, *alternative strings* seemed the best option.

The alternative styles track at the March 2003 conference drew standing-room-down-the-hall attendance for every clinic and jam session. We featured two dozen top players spanning sixteen styles. We all left the conference certain that the string community had turned an important corner in its evolution.

The inclusion of bowed string instruments in styles worldwide can be traced back for centuries in one form or other. We can thank the recording industry, the Internet, radio, television, publishers, and a handful of educational pioneers and eclectic performing artists for a growing interest in including the art of improvisation and multi-styles into the mainstream of string pedagogy.

Tradition

All music is the product of human imagination. We forget this too easily. Once codified into structures, imaginative ideas are all too often converted into rules and standards. Thus, instead of receiving the joy, gratification, and fun available to us every day when we make music, we are encouraged and even taught to press the experience into a comparative, competitive one.

Rituals, prescribed belief systems, and fear tactics are often the tools societies use to maintain the status quo and inadvertently or intentionally prevent change. Thankfully, societies also comprise people who are willing to rebel against stagnant repetition—who press against the tide and create new ideas. If their ideas are accepted and emulated, then they, too, become codified, leading to innovation and change. Let's look more closely at how culture, notation, and technology contribute to censoring or encouraging change.

Culture

There is a paradox built into human nature. We are interested in new possibilities, new approaches, and surprises, but we are also afraid of and even intimidated by change. Within each culture, the interaction between government, religion, and the designated function of music is apt to accentuate one tendency over the other.

Throughout history, kings, wealthy patrons, and conquerors have played major roles in holding composers and musicians to cultural agreements or rules. If you thought your head was going to be chopped off as a penalty for using the wrong ethnic scale in your composition, would you alter your composition in favor of playing it safe? Even the knowledge that you could be banned from performing, or perform to an empty house, for deviating from the cultural norm might persuade you to follow the standards of your time. (The story of the seventeenth-century *viola de gamba* player Monsieur de Sainte Colombe, as depicted in the 1991 film *Tous les Matins du Monde*, provides a powerful illustration of this predicament.)

Today, the parameters of popular music are heavily controlled by what will and won't be aired on radio. So many millions of dollars are invested in each new artist that record companies are hesitant to take the risk of signing truly creative artists who might challenge listeners' ears, and thus their own financial returns.

Notation

When tunes are taught by ear, it is up to the memory and taste of individual musicians to carry those tunes forward, each in a somewhat different way. If they forget sections, they can replace them with variations; if they don't remember how their mentors ornamented them, they can add a few embellishments of their own. On the other hand, if that same tune is written down and a student learns it by reading it, the melody is more likely to forever be cast in stone. Fiddle tunes are traditionally open to widely varying interpretations. However, even fiddle tunes that are played in unison encourage formulaic versions.

With compositions for ensembles or orchestras, it is understandable that the need to control each player's part is essential. If players have to keep returning to the written page to remember how the piece is "supposed to" sound, the likelihood of their adding their own touches when playing at home on their own time are dramatically reduced. The end result of this process is armies of musicians who cannot play a note unless they are looking at printed music.

Publishing and Technology

Go to a small village and record the music of the people there. Study it, categorize it, write a book about it, and name it. That music is now known for its signature traits and stands less chance of evolving.

To study traditional music properly would be impossible. We would have to dip into that same village once every fifty years or so (without anyone knowing that we were there), record the music, and, after about a thousand years, run a comparison of what had changed or remained the same. Then we would have to compare that information to similar information from another village a few miles away! This comparison would include such elements as:

+ tuning system
+ preferred tonal centers
+ number of notes and their configuration in the most popular scales (not every culture uses seven notes per scale)
+ structure (length, repetition, number of sections)
+ harmonic motion
+ ornamentation
+ rhythmic heartbeat
+ instrumentation
+ arrangement
+ function (work song, spiritual, dance, entertainment, self-expression, and so on)

To Trad or Not to Trad...

There has been an ongoing debate over whether it is politically correct to learn a traditional tune without simultaneously studying its culture and music in depth. Some players feel that we cheapen the music and show disrespect when we behave like bees, collecting drops of nectar and then moving on.

Somewhere in the Internet archives of a discussion group called Fiddle-L, you will find a maelstrom initiated by one fiddler's response to my book *The Contemporary Violinist*. His twenty-four-page essay in response to my four-page section on Irish fiddling exemplifies just how passionate traditionalists can be about remaining true to style: studying it in depth before attempting to play repertoire, and then sticking with that one tradition for life. (Ironically, the gentleman who submitted

A student once told me a story about his Balkan dance group. Members had learned a series of Balkan dances from a video of old-timers who had since passed away. They were very proud of helping preserve this particular district's dance traditions. They chose a local nursing home known for its concentration of residents from the Balkans and donated their time to perform the dances.

The residents were entertained and thanked the group after the show. But they also questioned why the performers had changed the dances so much. Of course, the group was quite shocked by this. When group members asked for greater detail, they were told that, in every dance, they had kept their feet too close to the ground. Apparently, the dances were meant to elevate the dancers from the floor. Putting two and two together, the members realized that the video was not quite as accurate a "time capsule" as they had initially assumed. In fact, the old-timers on the video had inadvertently misrepresented their own tradition, as they were too old to dance the dances the way they had in their youth!

the essay is an Irish fiddler of French origin, but his sentiment can be found in many traditional circles.)

The response to his post on Fiddle-L was met with a number of contrary opinions, including the following: that taking note of each genre by spending time learning a few tunes *is* a sign of respect, that it is fine to play for fun, that the most dedicated traditionalists within each style will always see to it that the authenticity of the style never dies, and so on.

It is important for you to consider these arguments when you decide how you want to present material to your students. In our own playing, there are those of us who simply want to taste and enjoy a number of genres, mastering the elements of the music that give us pleasure and skipping over some of the more detailed aspects of the music. Some of us originate our own forms of music, and others play everything they can from all over the world using a classical articulation of each style.

As educators, though, I maintain that we have a slightly different responsibility. We must do the best we can to respect each genre, explore its roots, and present that information to our students as we teach them the tunes of various traditions and cultures.

Who Decided What We Should Play?

Why do we place value on one form of music above another? For instance, have you ever wondered why most American and European musical institutions have chosen to ignore local genres in favor of the exclusive study of Western European classical music? Why has this been the case throughout the Southern states of America, where African-American slaves created the blues fiddle style and every town generated its own variation of old-time fiddling? Or in Texas, where Bob Wills helped innovate a vibrant style known as Western swing? How about Louisiana, where Cajun music was cooked up in the spiciest of pots? Consider, too, the United Kingdom and Scotland, where a rich Celtic tradition dating back at least ten centuries has influenced music in Spain, Canada, and the United States. The study of history and geography is required throughout our school systems, yet we tend to ignore rich musical traditions cultivated in our own backyards.

Juilliard has come a long way since I taught there. They now offer jazz and some contemporary music courses. When I was hired to teach Musicianship Through World Music for the Music Advancement Program (MAP) in the 1990s, I eagerly attended my first faculty meeting and reception. When introductions were made, a man in a high position at the school said, "Quite frankly, I don't know what you are doing here. We, at Juilliard, know our purpose. We are dedicated to perpetuating the study of Western European classical music." I was unprepared for his greeting, and quite astonished. While inwardly fighting disappointment and confusion, I managed to get my lips to reply, "In all conscience, I cannot teach young people that there is a hierarchy among the musics of the world. How can you say that there is nothing of value students can learn about the melodies, rhythms, scales, structures, theory, or practice techniques created by the rich musical imagination of all cultures?" He could not think of a good comeback, so he nodded abstractly and walked away.

Is it possible that ethnic, cultural, and economic elitism led to the institutionalization of a musical style—classical—which was often shaped and controlled by the upper classes of Europe? Money and power have their advantages when it comes to the support of more complex structures, whether architectural or musical. Through the use of a well-defined system of notation, rather than the aural tradition used by most other musical styles, classical music clearly evolved to offer an unparalleled interplay of complex and sophisticated melodic and harmonic lines.

Ironically, immigrants came to America in favor of building new lives free of censorship, yet carried beliefs and attitudes about music embedded so deeply as to not be noticed, questioned, or changed. Hillbilly or old-time music and the subsequent spin-offs of other fiddle styles were classified as the music of the uneducated, poor, or common folk, while classical was associated with the privileged. In an interview, pianist and conductor Leonard Bernstein described how his father did not approve of his pursuit of music. He felt that music was not an honorable profession, as his only associations were with the klezmer musicians of Europe. Thus he could only imagine a life of poverty and low status for his son. He was obviously wrong—both about his son and about klezmer music. Bernstein went on to achieve enormous success, which included helping validate jazz in the eyes of white America, and klezmer music has become so popular that even Itzhak Perlman tried his hand at it on his PBS special *In the Fiddler's House*.

Should the value of music be determined by the acclaim earned by one individual? By the size of the paycheck? By society's temporal values? Once we are able to answer all of these questions with a resounding "no," we will know that we have created a new foundation. We will assign value to the unique nature of each style of music, freed from old definitions.

Almost any classical devotee, once exposed to world music, will come to realize its value. Take, for instance, Yehudi Menuhin. He was acclaimed worldwide as a classical violinist and then went on in 1979 to author *The Music of Man*, a book acknowledging and embracing the wider roots and culture of music. Many heralded classical composers have dipped into the bountiful supply of soulful folk melodies when in need of inspiration. What, in societies' minds, has made their compositions or arrangements valid, but not the original source material? Contemplating this question is important, and essential to how you will develop your teaching curriculum. While considering the diverse population in your classroom, it is well worth taking the time to examine whether you want your program to be exclusive or inclusive.

For instance, some individuals believe that superior harmonic development automatically places classical music above every other music of the world. Here are just a few examples of specific attributes offered by other styles:

Western European classical music only has three or four functional rhythms—that is, meters that are in everyday use, such as 3/4, 4/4, and 6/8. It also has only a handful of functional scales: major, four kinds of minor, diminished, and augmented. India has over one hundred functional rhythms and hundreds of scales. African drumming sustains complex rhythmic cycles that gravitate around different downbeats, yet interlace perfectly into a complex musical tapestry. Jazz requires equal access to all twelve keys on (at least) seven primary chord types, each requiring a different scale or mode. One tune, such as the bossa nova "Wave" by Brazilian composer Antonio Carlos Jobim, can often require a performer to use over a dozen scales in order to improvise appropriately over the tune's harmonic structure. Bluegrass tunes may require continuously fingered double-stops, speed, shifts to all positions, a bowed rhythmic pattern called the shuffle stroke, and an improvised solo using all of these techniques after the melody has been played. Latin music offers a complex rhythmic world; Eastern European sports odd meter, alternating meter, and tempo changes; and we haven't even begun to discuss the deep spiritual values interconnected with each note of the Asians' pentatonic scale, their discovery of the mathematics behind justified intonation, and so on.

Clearly, a philosophical base that promotes condescension and competitiveness is the product of an older style of thinking that we must consider shedding at this point in human history. You have an opportunity to help foster a major shift in our educational system. As an educator, you are in the position to help create a system that embraces all cultures and their unique creative contributions to life and music.

Improving the Quality of Experience

While chatting with a Pilates instructor at my gym, I mentioned that I was a violinist. She said, "I used to play violin. I didn't sit in the very first chair of our school orchestra, but I was pretty good. My teacher told me that I wasn't good enough to be a professional, so I quit. After all, I wasn't a prodigy. I still have my violin. It is in my closet." When I asked her why she hadn't continued to play for the fun of it, she replied, "Oh, I didn't know I could. It just never occurred to me."

Early in life we are constantly bombarded with lessons from our parents, relatives, teachers, and spiritual or religious leaders about correct behavior, thought, speech, and organization of our activities. Add the quintessential classical training to the mix, with its juries, auditions, competitions, and hierarchy on the basis of playing skills and instrument value, and a mindset develops that emotionally positions us to expect instructions regarding what to do, how to do it, and when to do it. We come to consciously—or unconsciously—fear negative consequences for "breaking the rules," "making mistakes," or thinking for ourselves "outside the box." We become overly concerned with what people think about how we look and sound rather than focusing on the joy of creating music.

Ironically, some of the individuals we respect most in society have cultivated the ability to think outside of conventional conditioning. As you include alternative styles and improvisation into your teaching curriculum, you will have an opportunity to define the messages you wish to convey to your students. The tendency will be to bring the old mind-set with you into teaching and playing, so the conversion may not happen automatically.

The classical hierarchy has created an unattainable ideal, much like the glamour magazines that touch up and thin down their models digitally, causing teenagers to stop eating in an effort to live up to the aesthetic values that surround them. We have never had a system in place that defined the difference between the training and methodology designed to create a prodigy, soloist, or symphony musician versus a talented professional or an enthusiast. Most teaching techniques have built-in attitudes that it is not enough to be a child in love with music. That child must be pushed, rated, and made to form a love/hate relationship with his or her instrument. Almost all of us received similar messages, whether through a look on a teacher's face or an actual lecture. Lectures may have consisted of words such as "I wouldn't pursue it if I were you" or "I don't think you can earn a living," all amounting in our minds to "Give up."

Our primary role models for many decades consisted of a small circle of virtuoso male violinists. If we couldn't be like them, why bother to continue? And while it was thrilling to see female role models such as Midori and Anne-Sophie Mutter move to the forefront, for most of us, they still represented unattainable models.

Add up the number of prodigies we have seen on the violin, viola, and cello over the last four centuries. You may notice that the total list of names is rather small. These have been the primary role models for generations of classical string players. In folk music, children's role models might be their uncles, cousins, neighbors, or a stranger at the town dance—all of whom play for the love of it. It would be interesting to do a study on the numbers. We might predict that more fiddlers introduced to the violin during childhood play for life than classically trained kids in formal programs. The system is flawed and, I assert, must change.

It is essential for music education to emphasize playing for the sheer love of music and to be prepared to offer support to students who wish to be involved with music in a non-professional manner after they graduate. This includes putting them in touch with amateur orchestras, jam sessions, community music associations, and so forth.

> "I dream I am playing a Vivaldi concerto (unaccompanied) like what I did in my teens, for a violin competition. In line behind me are all teenage prodigies who are here to win (all girls with flower print dresses and bows). I am here to have the experience.
>
> "As I play the Vivaldi concerto, I can tell I'm rushing, the G string isn't sounding out, and I'm not shaping my notes very well. I feel afraid and very disappointed over how I sound. I see the three judges in front of me writing all these problems down (like I didn't know it already). And then near the end I completely forget the piece. I panic only for a second, but then I realize I can make it up. Instead of freaking out I improvise—in the style of Vivaldi. I finally totally let go and get into the music, sounding *so* much better, technically and emotionally, than before. I play exciting double stops, swoop from string to string, improvising all the way to a beautiful finale up high on the E string.
>
> "I'm so proud and exhilarated, happy and victorious. I notice that most of the people in the room didn't even notice it wasn't Vivaldi, or they thought I meant to do it as a cadenza. I see the three judges still scowling, giving me low marks and as many criticisms as possible, but I also see that there is one space for *improvise* on the ballot and I think I must get high marks in that. But now it doesn't matter what they think. I feel great."
>
> ***Rachel Farmer, freestyle violinist***

While it may feel almost impossible to imagine the act of making and teaching music as embracing a quality of experience different from the one you grew up knowing, one does exist. Folk fiddlers get together all the time to play at dances, jam sessions, and fiddle tune swaps. They even jam at fiddle competitions. They have the opportunity to experience a shared passion for music-making and a sense of community, acceptance, support, and friendship.

How do we take our first wobbly steps into a new paradigm? We have to trust that high standards can be taught and sustained through a love for the instrument. We must realize that we can turn the serious pursuit of technique into musical games— games that often accomplish even more than the old approach that converted "whistle while you work" into "suffer while you practice." We have to change the rules and open the doors. Promoting student involvement within the alternative string community can provide the opportunity to foster new attitudes within our educational institutions. As I see it, our choices are either to change the system or to lose future generations of musicians.

Why Integrate Other Styles into the Curriculum?

Those of us already teaching alternative styles have had the wonderful opportunity to see students come alive with interest, become more deeply involved in rehearsals, and practice with greater stimulation at home. Fiddling clubs have sprung up across America, thanks to the efforts of educators such as Bob Phillips, founder of Fiddlers Philharmonic. Projects including the Lakewood Project, where rock violinist Mark Wood worked with Beth Hankins's students to create a string rock show, keep students involved.

In high school and college residencies across the country, I always ask students what style of music they listen to most at home. Almost without exception, they say rock or pop. Out of a group of fifty, maybe one student has listened to blues or jazz (unless they are part of

"The idea was bold and innovative: to take instruments that had been played essentially the same way for hundreds of years and adapt them. Change them to create the sounds of a new generation. I felt it was my job as an educator to open that door and let students explore the areas that they wanted to explore. I think that's what teaching is all about: giving students opportunities to find themselves through the vehicles of their choice.

"The only vehicle that I had known was classical music. I had always listened to rock 'n' roll growing up in high school, but never had I thought of crossing the bridge of taking my string instrument and playing rock 'n' roll. Why can't we use rock 'n' roll instead of Bach to teach students how to play by ear, but still stay rooted in our techniques from four hundred years ago? To bring in an electric guitar and electric bass was an avenue that I felt legitimized the rock 'n' roll but also brought students into the group who didn't have a place in the school music program.

"They're willing to try new things. They're not afraid. They can't wait to get here. They can't wait to start playing. Their parents are calling me and telling me they can't get them to put their instruments away. That's what it is all about. It has become fun, it has become relaxing, it has become an outlet, which is what music should be."

Elizabeth Hankins, Director,
The Lakewood Project

a jazz program) and a few to fiddling if their music teachers have exposed them. The schism between what we are teaching teenagers and their primary musical interests may be costing us a whole new generation of string players and audiences. While it is our job to enable our students to appreciate classical music through exposure and its resulting familiarity—as well as, I maintain, to expose them to a wider musical panorama of styles—it is also important to keep them active on their instruments by showing interest in and respect for their musical taste.

Through listening to, discussing, and playing many different styles, your students will develop an appreciation for the

individual gifts offered by each genre. When you send out the message that differences enrich us as musicians and as people, and that neither homogenization nor hierarchy is the goal, you help your students recognize that we can live together with mutual respect for our

The Turtle Island String Quartet

differences. This, in turn, can make your students feel more recognized as individuals. After all, there is no such thing as a homogenous class in America—or anywhere in the world at this point in history—even where appearances indicate a shared racial background.

What Constitutes a Style?

What makes the music of one culture sound completely different from that of another? Even with a deep analysis of all of the individual elements that coalesce to create a style, there always remains an intangible element. Each culture has its own unique heartbeat, and no amount of analysis can reduce to words the entirety of what happens when sound and spirit intertwine. This is the beauty and power of music.

There are, however, a number of identifiable characteristics that coalesce to create a tangible musical fingerprint. The discussion of this topic can comprise a wonderful lesson or series of lessons you can present to your classes.

Each time you introduce a new style, present a master player from that genre on CD or video and challenge students to describe the music through some of the criteria discussed under National Standard number six (see page 23).

Notation falls short when it comes to the range of expressive dynamics that are actually available to musicians. Consider a line of eighth-notes as an example. On paper each note looks the same, yet in performance each can be lilted, dragged, swung, or cheated of its full time value. When teaching a new style, invite students to listen to a representative tune a number of times, even singing along with it, and guide them to pay attention as much as they can to how each note is articulated.

In addition to such musical elements as instrumentation, ornamentation, and meter, string players have five basic parameters to work with in each hand that will help define their sound. How we mirror or mix-and-match the activities of our two hands multiplies the spectrum of colors available to us from our sound palette. You can spend a few minutes of each class challenging your students to experiment with these parameters. Not only will this add depth and nuance to their technique and musicianship, it will increase their skill at recognizing what they hear on recordings or at live performances.

The Five Basic Parameters:

1. *Pressure*

   Subtle variations in pressure can greatly affect the expressive qualities of one's playing. To gain control over how the bow interacts with the string, students must learn to keep their hands flexible. All of the fingers need to be relaxed and curved. If a single finger is stiff, straight, or locked, it is extremely difficult to achieve subtlety of sound. Players then have to turn to the large muscles of the arm to regulate bow weight, which is an inefficient use of musculature.

2. *Speed*

Students should experiment with drawing fast long bows or slow short bows on notes with the same time values (making up for the time difference with appropriate rests) to create completely different expressive effects. Keep in mind that the closer the bow moves to the bridge, the greater the resistance of the strings. Therefore, players need to guide their bows closer to the bridge when moving slowly and further away when moving more quickly. Encourage students to experiment with bow speed and placement, and allow the resulting tonal variations to teach them where to place their bows when moving at different speeds.

3. *Duration*

Varying the length of time one holds a note, slides into it, or adds an ornament to it can also add a lot of flavor to one's playing. Learning how to change note length, yet not speed up or slow down the pulse of the music, is a challenge. If a player ends a note early, he or she must learn how to fill the extra space with silence; if a players holds a note slightly longer than written, he or she must compensate by slightly shortening the next note. The idea is to keep the overall measure or phrase length the same and to keep the pulse steady enough to dance to.

4. *Method of Entry,* and

5. *Method of Departure*

Students can practice paying attention to how they start and end notes and phrases, and experiment with the difference between staccato, legato, loud, soft, tapered (fade up, fade down), sudden changes, and gradual ones. This requires subtle control and they may get frustrated if they don't get the results they want immediately. Let them know that this kind of control takes time and practice. Try using images to assist them. For instance, instead of asking them to start a note pianissimo and make it gradually crescendo, ask them to describe the sound of a train from very far away that comes closer and closer, whirls by, and fades off into the distance.

Since arrangement and instrumentation help define style, play-ing a tune against varying rhythmic settings and instrumental accompaniments will change the overall sound of the per-formance.

To help your students understand how the same melody can be totally altered depending upon the context in which it is played, it can be interesting to teach, for example, an Irish tune, and then have students play that tune against different music-minus-one accompaniments, such as rock, calypso, and jazz. Encourage them to interpret the tune differently in response to the differ-ent rhythmic environment created by each accompaniments. You can use PG Music's computer software Band-in-a-Box to implement this educational experiment.

Meeting National Standards

You will be able to fulfill all ten national standards by includ-ing any one of the alternative styles discussed in this book into your curriculum. Certain styles will present new vantage points for your students. For instance, because orchestral music is harmonized, fiddling will give them an opportunity to play in unison. Unison playing on a short, repetitive melody such as a fiddle tune will enable weaker players to glimpse and grow into the future. They will hear the stronger players in a reinforcing manner.

In addition, students will have the opportunity to learn about musicians from their towns, states, or cultural backgrounds who created tunes that are still played today.

1. Singing, alone and with others, a varied repertoire of music

This standard appears to be directed to choral programs, but you can use vocal call and response as a starting point to teach unfamiliar rhythmic phrases, slide techniques, ornaments, and world scales to string players. The classical Indian music sys-tem teaches all musicians—including percussionists—through the voice first. An instrument's technical demands can often complicate and even slow down the initial learning process.

2. Performing on instruments, alone and with others, a varied repertoire of music

Varied is the key term here. Sometimes it is interpreted only to mean a score from a Broadway show tune, a movie theme, or the like. Unfortunately, musically or technically speaking, these scores do not require anything different from classical literature. Alternative styles give students opportunities to sample new grooves on their instruments, new left- and right-hand moves, and even a fresh interplay between the instruments.

3. Improvising melodies, variations, and accompaniments

Styles such as bluegrass, blues, rock, and jazz all incorporate improvisation in one manner or another. The suggested resources (books and videos) cited throughout this book will provide you with the warm-up techniques and exercises to explore a number of approaches to improvisation.

4. Composing and arranging music within specified guidelines

You can use a fiddle tune, which tends to have a shorter repetitive structure, as an easier entry point into composition than would be demanded by the classical genre. Students can also have a lot of fun trying to create a melody based, for example, on an unusual scale from another area of the world or a rhythmic motif from Afro-Cuban or African drumming.

5. Reading and notating music

Students will gain new skills as they read music from various cultures, and dictation can just as easily be given from an alternative piece as from a classical one. In fact, you can teach a fiddle tune by ear, thereby staying true to its aural tradition of learning, and then challenge your students to write the tune down.

6. Listening to, analyzing, and describing music

Comparing and contrasting several different styles helps focus the ears more acutely to the variables that come together to create a style:

+ tonal center
+ type of scale
+ preferred melodic intervals
+ preferred rhythmic motifs
+ meter
+ tempo
+ structure
+ unison (monophonic) or harmony (polyphonic)
+ ornamentation (left- and right-hand)
+ instrumentation (ethnic or Western, quantity of each instrument and ensemble size)
+ arrangement
+ rhythmic groove (unison or polyrhythmic)
+ phrasing (length of each idea, how entrances and exits are articulated)
+ emotional feel
+ dynamic feel

7. Evaluating music and music performances

Rather than drawing from a prescribed approach, you have an opportunity to invent an individualized class criteria by challenging each class to invent its own system of evaluation. What do students consider important standards for interesting, well-written, and well-performed music? Why?

8. Understanding relationships between music, the other arts, and disciplines outside the arts

With each stylistic unit you present, you have the opportunity to give students an overview of the culture that created that style. This includes any variables that might have influenced or shaped that style, such as language, government, visual art, and dance.

9. Understanding music in relation to history and culture

Teaching alternative string styles provides an opportunity to present information in relevant context.

10. Understanding dance as it relates to music

There is a corresponding dance for almost every fiddle style, and for many of the world styles. This presents you with a gold-mine of possibilities. Students can learn the Cajun two-step, a sixties versus an eighties rock 'n' roll dance move, a Western line dance, the tango, the mambo, or a square dance. From clogging to jazz tap-dancing, you can turn to Hollywood movie footage, dance videos, or guest specialists as resources.

Expanding Our Skills 3

"But That's the Way I Was Trained..."

From medicine to music, it takes hard work to excel in every highly evolved discipline. We enter our training process knowing little or nothing, often directed by an inexplicable passion. We must place our faith in teachers, institutions, and the collective process that co-created our field of study. We emerge with a degree or recognition, and from that point forward are less and less likely to want to start over or change our ways. After all, we have already made such a huge investment of time and effort.

We also live with a prevalent belief that the older one gets or the longer one has been doing something a certain way, the less possibility one has of learning anything new. Everyone appears to have subscribed to some kind of tribal idea that the six to twelve years it takes a young person to develop an acceptable level of competency on his or her instrument (having started from scratch) is an acceptable investment of his or her time. Yet this same tribe has agreed that the two to five years it may take an adult to learn a new style or how to improvise after already having played for years can only be an absurd pipe-dream. Have you ever stopped to examine the psychology behind this? Or the physiology?

If we can rebuild bone mass through weight lifting when we are in our seventies or eighties, and we can build new cells in our brain to accommodate new mental tasks at any time, then why can't we take a skill we already have and apply it in a new direction?

Cultural myths, such as "old dogs can't learn new tricks" or "I'm too set in my ways," gain strength over time. The greater the number of believers, the more times these slogans are repeated and the more deeply we believe them. But this doesn't mean that they are true.

Belief in a learning-related limitation is often a front for fear: fear of sounding bad in public, fear of loss of control, fear of failure. We tend to invest greater importance into status as we age, and the accepted pedagogical model dictates that the teacher must be an authority in the field at all times. Why not be great at what you already do while openly pursuing supplementary skills? You can become a wonderful role model to your students.

Learning something new later in your life process is in many ways easier, because your level of motivation is higher, your skill base is more finely developed, and your brain-to-muscle facility has been cultivated longer. If you are missing a necessary skill at this point in life, trying something new can give you the opportunity to strengthen your weak area.

Since we learn to speak and to make music by listening, an environment filled with music is conducive to faster learning. Facilitate your learning process and that of your students by listening as much as possible: to live concerts, in-school clinicians, CDs, and videos—whatever materials you can locate in whichever genre you decide to pursue.

As you probably already know, small consistent actions add up to create large-scale success. Many individuals sabotage momentum when they stop working on something new each time they doubt themselves or feel discouraged or afraid. They allow these feelings to slow them down or stop them altogether. These fear-based feelings come up for all musicians, but the player who practices more in the face of inner obstacles is the one who succeeds.

Changing one's inner language can be a powerful tool. Start by changing "I can't do it" to "I think I can't do it, but I'll try." Convert "I'm too old to change" to "I have another ten, twenty, thirty, or forty years ahead of me to learn how to do this." Focus on every success rather than every failure.

With today's medical breakthroughs, we can expect to live anywhere from eighty to a hundred years. With advancements in technology, we can now use these years to learn anything that appeals to us through at least nine vehicles:

+ private teacher
+ credited class
+ workshop
+ television
+ cassette
+ video
+ CD
+ DVD
+ Internet

The steps you take to master new skills and contend with whatever is impeding you from making progress will make you a better educator. Every roadblock you must personally explore and move beyond will give you the tools to help future students with similar impediments. It is never too late to learn something new. And if you don't work on attaining new skills, your loss will become your students' loss.

Dimensional Theory: Whole-Brain Learning

Our society has oriented the educational system towards left-brain learning. We learn facts in a linear (step-by-step) sequence. This is problematic, because, while our teaching methods present facts or skills that are essential, they are taught out of context. Knowing something and not being able to use what you know (or understand how it is relevant to music-making) can make the information useless and easy to forget.

In school, when we learn math and algebra, it is taught in a manner strangely disassociated from practical applications. Students can get straight A's in math, yet not have a clue regarding how many years it would take to pay back a credit card or how much interest they would have paid in that time. Those same students could go on to do their doctoral dissertations on divorce in America. They could have categorized the numbers, ethnic backgrounds, and number of years couples tend to stay together. Then they could get married themselves and not have a clue as to how to build a long-lasting, healthy partnership.

Music theory and technique are generally approached in this same abstract, academic manner. For instance, we tend to learn key signatures through memorization. We look at the sheet music and remind ourselves which notes to lower or raise, but we have not truly connected with the individual characteristics of that particular key over another one: the sound, the feel, or the right-brain map of it on our fingerboard.

In fact, after a typical music theory class, many students are able to correctly answer all of the questions on an exam but unable to apply what they have learned to their instruments. In traditional theory classes, students aren't taught a sequence of discovery, just a series of facts. They aren't taught to picture information on their specific instruments, but on a keyboard. They aren't asked on exams to come up with playing situations that would demonstrate how that information might be applied. Such information tends to get processed by the brain simply as facts to be memorized and filed away. This is because students are rarely led through a more practical process of hands-on musical discovery within which the relationship between theory and actual playing is discovered or illuminated.

We can approach alternative string styles using the same techniques we have learned through classical pedagogy, or we can change our curricula to employ more practical learning techniques. Whole-brain learning will help our students build stronger, more easily applicable skills. This approach involves presenting new information through four approaches, so that it is assimilated equally into four learning centers:

1. Hear it

Teach students to hear the notes of a melody before they play them on their instruments. This can be stimulated through call and response exercises, through learning tunes by ear first (rather than from printed music), or through singing each melodic phrase before playing it. Some brain researchers associate this skill with the right brain, others with the limbic system (the lower cortex, through which we funnel our five senses). Exercises such as those above stimulate an awareness of the spatial relationships between the pitches, routing the mental processes through the right brain.

2. Map it

Condition students to visualize the notes before they place their fingers on the fingerboard. This can be accomplished by calling out the string, the note, and the finger that will be used. Then ask students to close their eyes and picture playing that note. As students become more adept, you can move on to two notes, then three, and finally, whole phrases. You are now accessing their right brains, which are in charge of generating spatial pictures.

3. Name it

Link the auditory process (hearing the melody) and the imagistic process (visualizing playing the melody) with naming the notes, which is a left-brain skill. Ask students to pick a scale or the opening phrase to a piece of music. Then, one by one, challenge each student to sing that phrase while naming the fingerings and notes.

4. Perceive it in a structural context

Don't lose the forest for the trees: frame information in a larger context. Point out relationships as students learn new tunes. For instance, if a tune opens with the sequence A, F#, D, point out that this is the upside-down arpeggio of a D major chord. Theoretical information can thus be taught within the context of a musical activity. Analytical thought activates the left brain.

Eightfold Audiation

One might assume that all musicians anticipate the sound of what they are going to play before they actually play it. The mental facility we use to hear the melody in the inner ear before actually sounding it out is called *audiation*. Unfortunately, reading musicians can become so dependant on written music that they tend to hear what they have played only during playing or afterwards.

Neurology can now explain in minute detail exactly what happens when we decide to initiate an action. The thought triggers a series of chemical reactions that result in communication between the nervous system and specific muscular movements. This process comprises a complex relay station, yet results in an instantaneous response. Scientifically speaking, such a process can only occur one way. Yet the original thought command that initiates the nerve-to-muscle response can be facilitated in several ways.

Musicians who are trained through Suzuki or solfège stand a better chance of initiating motion through audiation. But even with the best-trained listen-first musicians, extensive reading can encourage the brain to bypass this hook-up in favor of building a series of coded muscle moves: symbol X on the page signals the muscles to move the bow like such; symbol Y signals the muscles to move the left hand like such; and so on. This mechanical orientation to playing can place the ears in the judge's seat: move, listen, judge, adjust. And on the whole, it tends to produce precision without soul.

The whole-brain learning process will help your students orient themselves to a listen-first hierarchy. You can also fine-tune students' audiation skills by directing their ears to more specific aspects of musicianship (see below). You may have to approach this through demonstration and analysis until they know what, specifically, they need to communicate to their inner ears before playing.

Audiation includes at least eight components:

1. melody (sequence of pitches)
2. rhythms (sequence of timed pitch-to-pitch motions)
3. tempo (the pulse or the groove)
4. tone (timbre)
5. pitch (intonation)
6. how the player enters into or initiates each note or phrase
7. how the player shapes each note or phrase as it is sounded out into space
8. how the player completes each note or phrase (dead stop, taper, swell, and the degree to which this is implemented)

We can also audiate (hear):

+ emotions
+ images
+ colors
+ dynamics

+ volume
+ texture
+ intensity
+ space between notes

Groove-Based Playing

Defining Groove

At first, a fiddle, blues, or jazz tune in the hands of a classical violinist almost always sounds bland and uninspiring. It is like a rocking chair without its rocker—and remains so until players learn how to deprogram their legato/vibrato tendencies and pulse the phrases according to the language of the style. Each style has its own unique rhythmic dance. If it doesn't make your blood sizzle or inspire you to tap your feet or rock your body, the essence—the groove—is missing.

Aside from the organic feel of a style, there are three crucial elements that help create the groove: rhythmic subtext, articulation, and the use of space between the notes.

Rhythmic Subtext

To feel and create a groove, one must listen for the subtext. Players actually have to train their ears to move beyond the melody, ornamentation, mode or scale-type, tonal center, harmonic motion, and structure to the heartbeat of the music, or the water that runs underground. In more literal terms, each style has a pulse that can rarely be found in the actual notated rhythmic figures, but flows continuously underneath. It is always felt by players who have cultivated this skill, and it is always present, even during rests and held notes. For instance, there is a constant triplet feel underlying swing music, a shuffle stroke under old time, a shuffle stroke with slightly different accentuation beneath Cajun, and so on.

Articulation

When teaching a new style, you can present an example on CD, encouraging your students to pay attention to how each note or phrase is carved or etched. Challenge students to listen, in particular, for the particular type of pulse, accent, hesitation, anticipation, swell, or note-to-note transition with which the music is infused. This kind of in-depth listening is challenging and helps stimulate a heightened awareness of detail.

You can also have students identify whether the melodic phrases are played precisely on the beat or slightly behind. For instance, in blues and jazz, the notes are articulated slightly behind the beat, while Latin figures create an interplay between syncopated phrases and notes that fall precisely on the beat.

Defining Space and Phrasing

When we notate a thread of eighth-notes, they all look the same on paper, regardless of the genre. However, depending upon that genre, they will be played entirely differently. In classical literature, eighths tend to be phrased as either legato, detache, or staccato. In blues, eighths have a syncopated feel; in Irish they are lilted; and in Scottish, they are played crisply.

Rhythmic phrasing is both heard and felt. It is also a spatial affair. Suggest that students think of each downbeat or tick of the metronome as a marker that divides space evenly. Point out that each genre fills that space differently. If we listen carefully, we might even hear details such as the following: "In the second phrase of the solo, the fiddler came in a sixteenth of a beat late, attacked the first note like a hit on a cymbal, and extended the note a split second longer than the end of the beat while making it swell. Then he played four eighth-notes consecutively, but only filled half the space that was allotted for each eighth-note," and so forth.

Challenge your class to listen to one phrase of music performed in whatever style you are presenting. Play the phrase a number of times, assigning one "listening task" for each repetition. (You can use a computer program such as Transkriber

"What about the rhythm? Keys, schmeys! What's all this talk about keys and scales and melodies? Aren't we forgetting that 'It don't mean a thing if it ain't got that swing'? The first thing I tell my class in workshops is that ninety percent of what I do when I improvise is done with the bow. It controls the groove, phrasing, dynamics, articulation, and more. Before we place a finger on a string we drill on rhythms, and we keep coming back to it even after a weeklong camp.

"And despite all that, my beginning students (no matter what age or level of ability)—when it comes time to take an improvised solo, they play the lamest junk: perfectly in tune notes and the right scales and the right chords, etc., but it has no relationship to the groove, and the phrasing is all messed up. With the exception of a rare handful of individuals that I've encountered over the last twenty-five years, everyone I hear in my classes is so rhythmically impaired they deserve special parking places. I have seen excellent string players who have been conducting orchestras for years who cannot keep a steady backbeat on the high hat for more than a few bars. If I was putting together my dream jazz workshop it would start with a semester of *dance* lessons. Then a semester of *drums* and *percussion*. Then a semester of *walking bass*. Then a semester of *piano*—rhythm comping mostly—melodies composed within chord shapes only, with a left-hand bass line—focusing on boogie woogie. Then pick up the violin or viola or cello.

"In my mind, the melody should be subservient to the rhythm. And when you start playing chromatically, keys start to disintegrate anyway. My campaign is based on this simple platform: *It is the groove!*"

Randy Sabien, jazz violinist

to slow down a solo or tune to spotlight details.) For instance, during the first pass students could simply notice the melodic notes; next they might focus their ears only on swells (including the timing of each swell, the intensity, and the die-off); then they could pay attention to accents. Invite them to identify adjectives that describe the phrase, the note-to-note motion, and the emotional content. You might even ask students to draw pictures of what they hear. This style of listening takes ear-training to new heights.

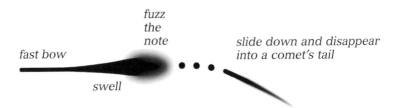

Creating a Groove

In the movie *Titanic*, the upper classes passively listened to classical music on the upper levels of the ship while the economic unfortunates partied and danced on the lower deck to the music of a fiddler. Historically, and throughout cultures worldwide, music has almost always been integral to dance or worship. From Scandinavian polskas to English quadrilles, Cajun two-steps, Viennese waltzes, Argentinean tangos, and American square dances, this partnership has challenged fiddlers over centuries to inspire millions of feet to move and groove, propelling dancers' bodies through the air.

In the classical genre, however, we have grown accustomed to staid audiences passively observing artists who function anonymously as servants to the composer. We have lost touch with music as a mobilizing force in our lives and lost the vibrant connection we could be helping our students create and feel as they play.

Most of the styles discussed in this book require a phased learning process:

1. Melody

2. Stylistically appropriate left- and right-hand ornamentation

3. Familiarity with structural elements such as length, repetition, harmonic motion (chordal accompaniment), and tonal center (key)

These elements are important—even essential—but without the proper feel, or groove, the tune may be played "correctly," yet lack spirit and sound bland. Mastering this concept is akin to learning a foreign language: one can learn vocabulary, the correct conjugation of verbs, and even proper pronunciation, but, until one finds the place inside where the dialect moves organically, one will sound like a foreigner.

It is important, as a part of the learning process, to expose students to as much authentic source material as possible. For instance, if you are focusing on Irish music, start each class by playing a few cuts from the CDs of respected Irish fiddlers. Also, whenever possible, use music-minus-one accompaniments. Start by restricting students to playing a single pitch repetitiously to the accompaniment's groove. When teaching old-time fiddling, for example, I ask students to play the shuffle stroke on open strings against an accompaniment for at least ten minutes before launching into the tune.

You can encourage your students to clap, tap, stomp, and walk the rhythms. Form a circle, put on a tune, and ask students to tap the pulse on one another's backs, so that they can practice connecting to the groove of the tune or accompaniment both by actually moving to it and by feeling it through physical sensation.

Doubling the Rhythm Section

Most string players are ill-prepared to play with rhythm sections. Solo performances, chamber groups, and orchestras each require a different type of listening. I often wonder to what degree a reading musician actually listens to the other parts at all. We are taught to count ourselves in and out and play with metronome accuracy, but how often do we really take the time to learn our accompanist's part or the ensemble's parts as meticulously as our own?

In alternative styles, the ensemble size and makeup of the rhythm section varies depending upon the style—from the acoustic guitar, mandolin, banjo, and bass used in bluegrass, to the trap set, piano, guitar, and bass in jazz. Whatever the style, the problem remains the same: many soloists don't have a clue about what members of the rhythm section are doing.

The brain needs specificity in order to better absorb events in real time. We would not expect students to be able to walk into a crowded room and recognize the face of someone they had

never met. Of course, they would easily be able to pick a familiar face out of a crowd. This applies to listening. Familiarity, and therefore the ability to identify and categorize melodic/rhythmic ideas, can improve the soloist's capabilities while playing.

Whenever making music with a rhythm section, no matter what the instrumentation or size, it is essential for musicians to practice listening carefully to the bass line—even learning to play it—as well as

Susie Hansen

to the other rhythm or melodic instruments' parts. It is often helpful to approach listening with questions such as: what are the other musicians generating rhythmically, harmonically, texturally, and expressively?

Most students are accustomed to listening to music as background ambience, whether it is coming from the radio, television, or CD player. Learning how to focus one's ears as if one were going to play the backbeat or harmonic motion oneself requires a completely different approach to listening. The cultivation of this kind of listening will improve ensemble interaction in any style of music.

Rhythmizing the Bow

There are two points we must focus on when preparing students to play alternative styles. In addition to teaching them how to accurately represent the style we are presenting, we must also teach our students to conceive of the bow arm as a rhythm instrument. This concept is still fairly new to classically trained players, and even to some alternative string players. We are dealing with a tradition in the making: a living, organic evolution of new bow techniques. The development of an independent, rhythmically complex use of the bow while phrasing a melody or improvising requires new training methods.

"For me, understanding how to approach bowing in Latin (Afro-Cuban) music was a gradual process that came from being immersed in the music for several years. The process involved not so much learning a different way to bow, but slowly coming to understand how the phrasing of the violin lines, particularly the *montunos* or vamps, were based around the subtle rhythms of the music (specifically, the *clave*, a two-bar rhythmic pattern). It also took a while to fully comprehend the aesthetic behind the music, which, of course, affected my technical approach. What makes an unfamiliar music 'work' is frequently very subtle and for the violin, usually has a lot to do with the bow arm."

Sam Bardfeld,
***jazz violinist and author,* Latin Violin**

Most string players have astonishingly underdeveloped capabilities when it comes to hearing and articulating sophisticated or "talking" rhythms with the bow hand. These include rhythms that are syncopated (versus evenly tempered), varying (versus repetitive), and groove-related (versus straight). Constant preoccupation with intonation, an emphasis on playing and learning music through the eyes, and the exclusion of focused rhythmic ear training have intersected to create a right-hand-serves-the-left relationship. In addition, classical players' attachment to legato sounds increases their reticence to explore new patterns of motion.

If you have a leg that you tend to lean on and use more, and you go to the gym and use an exercise machine that requires both legs, the stronger leg will always take over, perpetuating the existing hierarchy. In the case of playing an instrument, the stronger brain center (pitch) will dominate the weaker one

"When it comes to playing rhythm, I teach my students what I call 'controlled noise.' I have them start by playing a sixteenth-note pattern that incorporates two sixteenth-notes on the string, then one 'silent' sixteenth in the air, followed by the fourth sixteenth on the string. The bow moves up and down a full stroke regardless of whether or not the note is sounded out. Then I have them play one silent note (on a down bow), followed by three on the string, then one silent alternated with one on the string, etc., until we've covered all possible four-note combinations. After practicing the silent note approach, I have them substitute a 'chop' (controlled noise) for each silent note. The upbow right after the 'chop' is played (actually 'pinched') from off of the string cleanly along with the other two clean notes in the pattern. For this, I use double-stops, usually a fifth. The bow becomes analogous to the rock rhythm guitar player's pick; i.e., the 'air' notes that are now played 'on the string' should eventually transform into a discovery of mine: 'squeezed chops.' The left hand in this case, both on guitar and fiddle, is critical to the groove's success. The down chop is typically simultaneous to the left hand making a small dampening squeeze on the strings; the left hand then 'releases' on the successive up bow. These mufflings by the left hand actually help shape the groove."

Richard Greene, bluegrass fiddler

(rhythm) when one uses both hands to play. Since different brain centers power these skills, bowing exercises that are highly repetitive—articulating a single rhythmic phrase over and over again while the left hand plays a melodic line—tend to teach the right hand to be a drone, thereby re-strengthening and re-validating already strong left-hand skills. The consequence? Weaker independent control and articulation on the right side.

If an athlete keeps doing the same workout every day, at first the muscles will feel challenged, tired, and at times sore or stiff. Each incremental increase in strength will produce more energy. Results will be achieved up to a certain point in time, and then, gradually, the body will acclimate itself until the athlete becomes stuck on a plateau. At that point, the muscles are no longer being challenged: they will have physiologically adapted to expectations. Ironically, the tendency to change at this point is small, because the individual feels comfortable. Gains are being enjoyed—over and over and over again!

How do we train muscles to be stronger? We single out the weaker ones and use the element of surprise to challenge them. It is important to note that whichever cognitive orientation or muscle you train the longest will become the natural control center out of which your brain will initiate activity. Brain survival requires economy of motion; therefore, in your brain's world, it is not beneficial to rewire every time you want to do something new. The brain is designed to utilize the same pathways again and again. If players wish to develop the rhythmic center of their brains to the same extent as the left motor cortices (which are in charge of muscle move-

Rhythmic Practice Techniques

Before playing new rhythmic lines, it is helpful for musicians to first sing the rhythm, then tap it, and finally start playing at a slow tempo, increasing the speed only when they feel relaxed and are able to breathe deeply while playing the rhythmic pattern. Rhythmic exercises are meaningless unless played against a metronome or musical accompaniment, because students must learn to articulate rhythmic patterns against genre-specific accompaniments to prepare them for realistic playing situations.

ments on the right side of the body), they must be presented with new and constantly stepped-up challenges. This requires occupying the left hand with less or no activity while exercising the right in new ways.

Improvisation requires spontaneously creating a melodic line over harmonic changes while articulating the bow in rhythmically sophisticated ways. If you plan to teach blues, swing, jazz, popular music, bluegrass, or any other style that requires improvisational skills, include some genre-specific isolated right-hand warm-ups into your lesson plan to help your students cultivate new skills. If you skip this step, even as students become more adept at playing over the harmonic structure of the styles at hand, their rhythmic phrasing will remain stale and uninteresting.

Challenge students' bow hands by having them play repetitive, rhythmic warm-ups involving only open strings. If players use bowings that are not symmetrical, they have to track their bow arms more carefully. Each time your students acclimate and are able to do an exercise easily—which means their minds are beginning to go to sleep and "let their muscles do the walking"—it is time to create a new variation on the pattern to deepen the challenge.

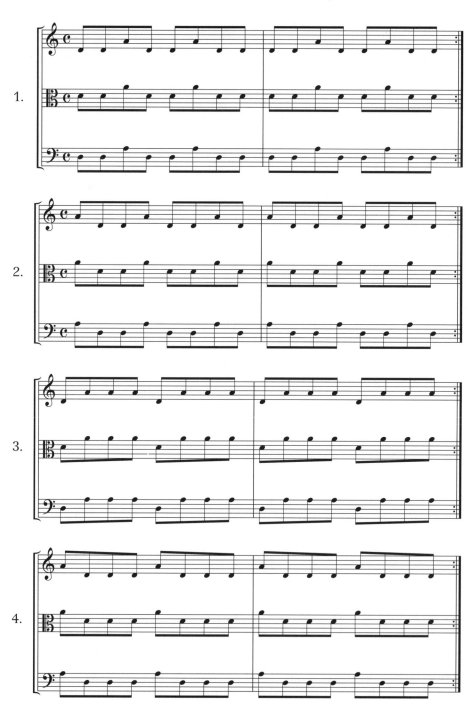

5.

Next, ask them to continue the right-hand pattern while adding in simple, repetitive left-hand scales or figures that do not involve reading from sheet music. As the challenges are increased on the right side, it is useful for players to articulate each new bow pattern on the open strings before once again adding in simple repetitive lines with the left.

Patterns that incorporate a series of repetitive upbows will help players avoid the common default mechanism of starting every improvisational phrase on a downbeat with a downbow. Upbow exercises can also be placed on the "and" of each beat, which helps players develop a feel for syncopation. Encourage students to make clean stops on each upbow without sounding stiff or unmusical:

The above exercise enables players to feel and accentuate the upbeat until it becomes a part of their hearing. To further mastery of syncopated rhythms it is also effective to move a melodic pattern across a key using a syncopated figure. For instance:

Accustom students to playing rhythmic units of three against two by using a pattern that is grouped in two units of three and one unit of two melodically, yet uses eighth-notes, which are rhythmic units of two. Have them carry this pattern across the four strings using the scale tones of the key of G to get started. Then challenge them to try other scales:

You can also invite students to sing in two (top line) while bowing in groups of three (bottom line):

Support Materials

📼 *Bluegrass Fiddle* by Richard Greene

Greene shows a myriad of bluegrass bowing patterns and techniques on this video: crossbowing, "separate" bowing, the bounced bow (spiccato), hemiola (accenting off beats), the "Georgia shuffle," and rhythm chopping. (Homespun Tapes)

📼 *Swingin' Jazz Violin* by Matt Glaser

With relaxed good humor, Glaser fills his video lesson with music theory, technical tips, and fascinating information on all aspects of swing/jazz music. As students play along with him, they will learn the basics of musical theory: playing in a circle of fifths; improvising around dominant seventh chords; using symmetrical structures (diminished, augmented, and whole tone scales); rhythmic accenting and articulation; bowing patterns; phrasing; and—most important of all—how to swing. (Homespun Tapes)

📼 *A Fiddle Lesson with Natalie MacMaster*

On this video lesson, one of Canada's greatest fiddlers and most dynamic performers teaches five traditional tunes, each in a different style. She breaks each tune down phrase by phrase, demonstrating the placement of the various drones, double-stops, cuttings of the bow, and other embellishments of the Cape Breton fiddle style. Her special emphasis is on the ornaments—grace notes, double grace notes, trills, pull-offs, hammer-ons, and so forth—and the bowing that is specific to each type of tune. She even touches on the clogging-style footwork that provides additional rhythmic emphasis for this dance music. (Homespun Tapes)

🔘 *Techniques for the Contemporary String Player: Part One, The Bow Hand* by Julie Lyonn Lieberman

This video features four essential bow control techniques, ten approaches to rhythmizing the bow, contemporary techniques to make each note speak, and much more! (Huiksi Music)

🔘 *Rhythmizing the Bow* by Julie Lyonn Lieberman

This video is chock full of rhythmic bow patterns from around the world. With special guests, Lieberman addresses rhythmic patterns of two against three, asymmetrical bow patterns, string crossing, clipped bows, chop technique, odd meter, fiddle bowings, and much more. (Huiksi Music)

How Does Improvisation Figure In?

Most string educators share a common concern: "I can't improvise, so how can I possibly teach my students?" Some teachers have tried to introduce improvisation, only to find that students are resistant. Student players share the same concerns as their teachers: fear of looking and sounding inept; fear of making a mistake; lack of knowledge as to how to proceed. As a result, everyone concerned finds it more convenient to bury the pursuit, and many string educators opt for an easier process: including alternative string scores in an orchestral format without attempting to address improvisational skills.

However, if the only way a musician can play his or her instrument is to stare at dots on a piece of paper, something is terribly wrong. Bach improvised. Classical Indian musicians improvise. Pygmies in the rainforest improvise. Eastern European musicians improvise. If the West is so tremendously "sophisticated," then why can so few of our musicians spontaneously create music on their instruments?

Improvisation trains the player to create a listen-first rather than a look-first hierarchy; to think structurally; to audiate. Improvisation cultivates creative thinking and listening. It engenders originality, which in turn promotes higher self-esteem. If you want students to learn that they can accomplish anything, you could send them on a fifty-mile hike. Alternatively, you could teach them how to improvise.

There are much easier ways to get started with improvisation than through the usual route of blues or jazz tunes, where the student has to track chords and scales while simultaneously attending to structural and stylistic concerns. I provide over one hundred games and techniques in my book *The Creative Band and Orchestra*. There are as many approaches to improvisation as there are styles in the world.

Four Approaches to Improvisation

1. Melodic improvisation

A number of folk styles focus on playing the melody repetitively. It is permissible, however, for each artist to bring his or her unique perspective into the rendition of each tune, through variations in bowing, ornaments, and dynamics. In this context, the art of improvisation involves such skills as timing, ornamentation, instrumentation, and phrasing.

When using melodic improvisation, rather than trying to emulate the original intentions of the composer, the player searches for just how that particular tune lives in his or her imagination. Having said this, there are many examples of contemporary fiddlers who, after playing the original melody, proceed to improvise using the notes of the key and certain stylistic attributes. They stray away from the melody of the tune and then return to it for closure. For instance, on her CD *Wild Blue*, Irish fiddler Eileen Ivers uses a traditional tune as a springboard for a marvelously wild improvisation with congas and guitar—two instruments that obviously are not used in traditional Irish music. Her rendition of the melody is authentic and soulful. She brings that same essence into her improvisation.

My little nine-year-old fiddle student took her first improvisation lesson two weeks ago and returned for her second lesson last night. She had taken the accompaniment track on the CD I'd made for her and had come up with a couple of her own melodies. She's really into the improvisation thing and is doing very well. Last night we put on a jazz improv track and now she is doing cartwheels, she is so excited! She immediately recognized the flatted third without my even mentioning it. We also did play some pieces that she has been working on from the Suzuki repertoire, but it is clear that her interest has really shifted toward improvisation. She loves it. We don't have a fixed lesson length and usually work until she gets tired. Since we started improvisation, I am the one who is getting tired! She just wants to play and play!

Curt Childress, Director, Effingham Youth String Music Program, Effingham, KS

2. Improvisation based on tonal center

In Eastern European and Indian pieces, the player draws upon the melodic and rhythmic feel and the scale upon which the melody is based as the foundation for improvisation. As a first step into improvisation, you can teach your class a scale and encourage each student to make up a short melody using its notes. You have a wonderful opportunity here to introduce scales from other cultures. In my book *Planet Musician*, you will find scales from around the world.

3. Riff-oriented improvisation

African melodies use short, repeating phrases (*ostinatos*) as accompaniments to the melody or improvisation. For string players, this is a treat. Inventing a rhythmic melodic phrase challenges students to become the rhythm section—definitely a skill most string players lack—and gives you an opportunity to introduce features such as syncopation, odd meter, and other complicated rhythmic elements as you help students develop more complex ostinatos.

4. Improvisation over chord changes

Blues and rock present the simplest harmonic structures you can use to introduce your students to playing over chord changes. Playing while paying attention to harmonic motion is the most challenging approach to improvisation, because players must keep track of where they are in the structure and must change keys or chordal scales in accordance with the chord changes. It is often easiest to start with two chords, having students practice moving back and forth between them, before going on to more advanced structures. The use of accompaniment for improvisation is essential. (See chapter 8, "Tools In the Classroom and Out.")

Removing the Stigma of "Right" and "Wrong"

Most students have been conditioned to fear mistakes. You can teach them a new mental/emotional framework by constantly reinforcing the tenet: "If it sounds good, then you're on the right track. If you don't like how it sounds, play it again and then change it." When a student grimaces over a line he or she has played, put this to use by asking the whole class to play the line three times. It is a good ear-training exercise and can stimulate an analysis of why those particular notes were displeasing. You can actually respond to the soloist's grimace by commending him or her for hearing that the notes didn't work. Most of the time, undesirable pitches are due to dwelling on scale rather than chord tones or to playing accidentals unintentionally. This provides a wonderful opportunity to review the scale called for by the piece and emphasize the importance of knowing the chord tones of the key.

Where Do I Start?

Since each individual in the classroom is unique, each class forms a different group chemistry. An activity that bombs with one class may be the favorite of the next. You will achieve a

"Improvisation in music has taught me a lot about fear and taking risks.

"Fear used to stop me from trying anything new. I would just find some way to chicken out or procrastinate. Learning to improvise on the violin has changed risk-taking from a paralyzing fear into a thrilling practice.

"In my experience, learning to overcome fear did not mean that I didn't feel it anymore. Instead, I learned to use it as information. Fear is no longer a concrete wall. It is a holograph of a wall! Learning to challenge that wall creates a different perception of it. Through improvisation and applying its principles within my life, a music lesson has turned into a life lesson."

Helen Yee, improvising violinist

John Blake, Jr.

higher success rate if you tailor to each group how you introduce new styles and techniques. It is helpful to first expose students to an overview of the possibilities, make a note regarding which styles most appeal to that group, and start with those styles. Often, once the students become involved and enjoy success, they will begin to show interest in styles they had formerly rejected.

Use the resource materials and discographies suggested throughout this book to pick out CDs to use for demonstration in each genre. You can play CDs by groups such as the Calgary Fiddlers, Barrage, or Fiddlers Philharmonic—three examples of student string classes that went on to successfully record and perform in numerous styles. You can also access the Internet to help you search out specific scores in various genres.

In classical training, we often use scale and etude books to help prepare students for the technical demands of the concerto. In non-classical styles, warm-ups can include style-specific patterns, rhythmic motifs, and bowings. For instance, if preparing students to play an old-time tune, you might ask them to first play the shuffle stroke (an old-time rhythmic bow pattern) on open strings against a rhythmic accompaniment, then apply the bowing to the scale tones of its key, next practice bowing some of the double-stops from the piece, and finally launch into the tune. This will give students an aural and physical warm-up before engaging their eyes. You can refer to my books *The Contemporary Violinist* and *Improvising Violin* for specific style-oriented warm-ups.

American Fiddle Styles *4*

H istoric Overview

The violin's popular role in American music may originally have been based on the accessibility of its parts and how easy and light it was to carry. Whether transported by boat from Europe by Scots-Irish immigrants or built on American soil, it maintained a central position in folk and classical music alike in the early days of the New World. Only wealthy immigrants could afford to bring a larger instrument such as a piano by ship. Rich and poor musicians alike could easily travel with a fiddle. In fact, early fiddles were small enough to tuck into one's suitcase or bag before being replaced in the 1800s with the size and design we enjoy today.

Thousands of tunes imported from the Celtic tradition were only as consistent as the memories of the fiddlers who traveled to America. The evolution of the repertoire was often determined by where immigrants chose to settle. In the mountains of Appalachia, where small communities were cut off from the advancements of the coast, traditions remained insular. Port cities invited a lively exchange and subsequent transformation of tunes, as did historic events that activated resettlement or migration, such as the gold rush West or, later, the Civil War.

Every village or town had its good players, and they played the old tunes whenever folks got together. A regional style developed for each area. When an itinerant musician traveled through with an unfamiliar new way of playing, tunes and playing techniques were swapped. New ideas were reworked into old tunes, which were, in turn, shared with others and carried on to new regions where they had never been played. Fiddling reflected the country as a whole: it was a melting pot for the consciousness of diverse populations, traveling to and throughout America for diverse reasons. It isn't surprising, then, that a number of new styles developed from this constant process of transformation. These included Cajun, old-time, bluegrass, Franco-American, Western swing, and a vibrant string band tradition, all of which evolved on American soil.

Many of the old fiddle tunes did not use standard tuning (G, D, A, E). Old-time fiddler Bruce Molsky, who has collected many authentic tunes, uses roughly fifteen different tuning systems. Some instruments were handmade out of cigar boxes or only had one string on them. Unfortunately, as was the case with styles such as the blues, the quirky original and diverse qualities of early tune form became standardized over time as well. There are still some "crooked tunes," as they are called, in French-Canadian fiddling.

At the start of the second half of the twentieth century, media evolved, especially the phonograph and radio, and began to eradicate the more pronounced regional stylistic distinctions. The proliferation of fiddle contests was no doubt a primary factor in eliminating differences as well. Judging, by its sheer nature, defines and enforces a set of aesthetic standards. The gradual shift in emphasis throughout the United States from playing for dances to playing at fiddle competitions has also changed the emphasis from the fiddler as rhythmic inspiration at social functions to fiddler as showpiece.

Violin or Fiddle: What's the Difference?

The terms fiddle and violin are interchangeable. There is no physical difference between the instruments. The only thing different is the material that is played on them. Occasionally folk fiddlers file their bridges slightly flatter to create greater ease when playing double-stops, and bluegrass fiddlers tend to prefer steel strings. And of course, there are a lot of jokes floating around that compare the two instruments musically. Fiddlers definitely do not call their instruments violins, because that would imply that they can't play the fiddle authentically. In fact, there is just as much snobbery from fiddlers toward classical players as there is from classical players toward fiddlers.

Why Create a Fiddling Club?

Fiddling provides a highly rhythmic, group-oriented activity. The sheer act of creating music in unison with other musicians provides a sense of belonging, mutuality, and safety. Young people, as well as adult beginners, are often able to have a taste of success more quickly on a fiddle tune than on a classical piece of music. This is the case for several reasons:

✦ The melody of a fiddle tune is short and repeated again and again, whereas that of a clas-

What's the difference between a fiddle and a chain saw?

You can turn a chain saw off.

Why did the fiddler cross the road?

It was the chicken's day off.

What's the difference between a fiddler playing in "D" and a locksmith?

A locksmith knows how to change keys, and can get paid for it.

Why are fiddles better than guitars?

They burn longer.

What's the difference between a fiddle and a Harley Davidson motorcycle?

You can tune a Harley.

What's the difference between a fiddle and a violin?

No one minds if you spill beer on a fiddle.

What's the difference between a violin and a fiddle?

A fiddle is fun to listen to.

"Haven't I seen your face before?" a judge demanded, looking down at the defendant.

"You have, your Honor," the man answered hopefully. "I gave your son violin lessons last winter."

"Ah, yes," recalled the judge. "Twenty years!"

Fiddle Tune Forms

air: a rubato instrumental song-like melody that is usually played slowly

breakdown: a general term applied to up-tempo old-time and bluegrass tunes in 2/4 and 4/4

country rag or *novelty rag*: a longer form (from three to five sections) using swung eighth-notes and syncopation; usually shaped over harmonic progressions like II-V-I or I-VI-II-V or even IV-#IVdim-I-VI-II-V

crooked tunes: a term used to describe a tune written with an uneven number of beats or measures; usually associated with French-Canadian fiddle tunes

double shuffle: a fiddle bowing that crosses the strings, striking a low double-stop twice and an upper double-stop once repetitively in an eighth-note pattern

hoedown: synonymous with "breakdown"

hornpipe: a medium-tempo tune that lilts its eighth-notes (they are notated as dotted rhythms) and moves more slowly than a reel

jig: a tune in 6/8 (double jig) time or 9/8 (slip jig) and built on an AABB structure; the single jig uses a quarter-note/eighth-note alternation, whereas the slip jig opens each measure with a quarter-note/eighth and then fills the rest of the measure with eighth-notes

march: a piece played at a walking tempo in 2/4 or 6/8 and commonly used for weddings or military processionals

continued →

sical piece tends to be lengthy and is performed only once.

✦ The memorization of a fiddle tune is reinforced through the group learning process, whereas a classical piece is played solo or within a section against other parts.

✦ Violin, viola, and cello all play the same melody in unison on a fiddle tune, which reinforces improvements in intonation more quickly than learning to adjust one's pitch alone or against harmonized orchestral parts.

✦ Finally, in contrast with classical music, fiddle tunes tend to stay in first position. They are also highly rhythmic, generating a great deal of energy, which keeps students engaged and interested.

Old-Time Fiddling

Victor Records made the first "old-time" recording in 1904. Most professional musicians didn't like the common names for this style—"hillbilly," "country," or "mountain music"—and therefore welcomed the new name coined in 1927 by Victor Records. Old-time fiddling came from the hands that built America, white and black alike. It evolved from Irish and Scottish fiddle tunes, English ballads, and Sea Chanties. Later, in some regions, syncopated rhythms incorporated by black blues fiddlers influenced the music.

The folk revival movement of the 1960s and a series of old-time fiddlers' associations that sprang up throughout the United States in the seventies helped preserve this tradition.

Some historic old-time fiddlers of note include Jim Bowles, Charlie Bowman, "Uncle" Norm Edmonds, Ed Haley, Eddon Hammons, Thomas Jefferson Jarrell, Emmett W. Lundy, Henry Reed, Alexander "Eck" Robertson, John Morgan Salyer, Hobart Smith, John L. "Bunt" Stephens, and William Hamilton Stepp.

Stylistic Characteristics

Most old-time tunes are built on an AABB form, with each section lasting either four or eight bars. Tunes are played anywhere from three to more than half a dozen times, depending on the player or the group. Authentic fiddlers rarely play the melody exactly the same way each time; rather, they add their own signature left- and right-hand ornaments and vary the melody slightly from repetition to repetition. The melody tends to stay true to its tonal center, so it is

Fiddle Tune Forms *(continued)*

longways: a line-facing-line dance tune

polka: a tune in 2/4 based on a sprightly dance that originally came from Eastern Europe and utilizes the same rhythmic structure as the shuffle stroke: an eighth-note followed by two sixteenths played repetitiously

polska: a Scandinavian dance form played in 3/4 with the accent on the third rather than the first beat

quadrille: a Franco-American dance form originally derived from a French dance in 2/4 or 6/8

quickstep: a tune similar to a reel, but originally intended for marching, played in 2/4 or 4/4 with a "quick step"

reel: a tune built on an AABB structure in 2/4 or 4/4 and made up of run-on eighth- or sixteenth-notes

set-tunes: cut-time tunes for set or square dancing

Schottische: a Scottish dance in 3/4 time

strathpey: a relative of the hornpipe, played at a slower tempo in 4/4 time and using dotted rhythms

waltz: a 3/4 time dance tune

extremely rare to hear any accidentals. The keys tend to reside in G, D, A, and E major or minor, and the bow arm actively crosses back and forth between the four strings. Open strings are used to drone against (if these strings are compatible with the chord tones of the key).

Old-time players must have command over a series of genre-specific bowings, such as the shuffle stroke, the Georgia shuffle, and the double shuffle (which involves a fast, repetitive string-crossing). They also must be skilled at accentuating notes within each phrase.

Shuffle stroke

Georgia shuffle

Double shuffle

Artist Sampler

Thomas Jefferson (Tommy) Jarrell (1886–1975)

Jarrell was born in North Carolina. His family farmed, and he started to work the fields at an early age. When he was seven years old, a farmhand, Bauga Cockerham, taught him his first tune on the banjo; about a year later, his father bought him his own banjo. At thirteen, Jarrell began to play on his father's fiddle. A year later, in 1915, he bought his own fiddle for ten dollars. Jarrell's fiddle is now part of the Smithsonian Institute collection in Washington, D.C.

Jarrell recorded seven albums. He performed at colleges and universities throughout the country, the Smithsonian Institute in Washington, D.C., and many festivals. In 1982, he was selected as one of the fifteen master folk artists in the first National Heritage Fellowships of the National Endowment for the Arts. He received a certificate and monetary award at a ceremony at the annual American Folklife Festival in Washington, D.C. A film about Jarrell, *Sprout Wings and Fly*, can be purchased on video.

♫ *Listen for*
Driving rhythm; soulful playing style; rough tone

Support Materials

📼 *Visits with Tommy Jarrell: Solo Fiddle and Stories*
> This three-volume video set features interviews, autobiographical material, and dozens of tunes that display Jarrell's rhythmic bow patterns. You will even see Jarrell's dog, Bolliver. (Palmer Media)

💿 *Discography*
Jarrell, Tommy, *The Legacy of Tommy Jarrell, Vol. 1, 2, and 3* (County)
Jarrell, Tommy, *Best Fiddle and Banjo Duets* (County)
Jarrell, Tommy, *Sail Away Ladies* (County)

Bruce Molsky (b.1955)

photo by Irene Young

Bruce Molsky is at the forefront of reinvigorating some of the unique fiddle styles of the southeastern United States. He can be considered a revivalist, but has dug so deeply into the tradition that he may be said to have gained access to the fountain of tradition. One of the most influential fiddlers of his generation, Bruce Molsky is also a remarkable guitarist, banjoist, and singer. His high-spirited music melds the archaic mountain sounds of Appalachia with the power of blues and the rhythmic intricacies of traditional African music. The *Minneapolis Star-Tribune* has called Molsky "old-time music's answer to Ry Cooder—a commanding musician with a voracious appetite for traditional music styles." Darol Anger has dubbed him "The Rembrandt of Appalachian Fiddling." Molsky insists above all that music must be fun and engaging.

Renowned musicians Tommy Jarrell and Albert Hash were two of Molsky's mentors in the Blue Ridge Mountains, where he first learned to play. Thanks in part to his time spent with these old masters, Molsky has earned numerous awards at fiddle and banjo contests throughout the South, including Galax, Virginia; Mount Airy, North Carolina; and the Appalachian String Band Festival in West Virginia.

𝄞 *Listen for*

Solid vibrant groove created by the bow; sounds as rich as a cathedral; impeccable intonation; traditional yet contemporary personality

💿 *Discography*

Molsky, Bruce, *Lost Boy* (Rounder)

Molsky, Bruce, *Poor Man's Troubles* (Rounder Select)

Molsky, Bruce, *Bruce Molsky and Big Hoedown* (Rounder Select)

Additional Support Materials: Old-Time

📖 *Appalachian Fiddle* by Miles Krassen

This book features transcriptions of fifty-eight grand old fiddle tunes. (Music Sales Corp.)

📖 *Beginning Old-Time Fiddle* by Alan Kaufman

More than forty tunes for the absolute beginner are presented in this book. (Music Sales Corp.)

📖 *Bruce Molsky: Lost Boy* by Bruce Molsky

There is some wonderful playing on *Lost Boy*, the CD from which this book is drawn. The book provides detailed transcriptions that will give fiddlers an idea of what the great performers do. It also can act as a springboard to their own interpretations of these tunes. The fiddle solos from the CD are transcribed, with lyrics included. (Mel Bay Publications)

📼 *Carrying on the Traditions: Appalachian Fiddling Today*

This two-hour video features eight great Appalachian-style fiddlers: Charlie Acuff, Ralph Blizard, Dan Gellert, Bruce Greene, John Hartford, Brad Leftwich, Kirk Sutphin, and Red Wilson. (Fiddler Magazine)

📼 *John Hartford's Old Time Fiddling* with John Hartford

In this video, Hartford discusses and demonstrates bowing styles and left-hand techniques. He also teaches a number of important old-time tunes. (Elderly Instruments)

📼 *Learning Old-Time Fiddle Appalachian Style* with Alan Jabbour

Alan Jabbour teaches ten easy pieces in this instructional video. He deconstructs Upper South old-time fiddling, explaining its bowings and syncopation patterns, as well providing an inset bowing "window." The video (also available on DVD) includes cross-tunings, a half-hour interview about fiddling with Jabbour, and transcriptions. Jabbour performs the tunes up-to-speed, slow, and at a medium

tempo, to make the notes, bowings, and ornaments easier to follow. (In the Groove Workshops)

📼 *Learn to Play Old-Time Fiddle* taught by Brad Leftwich

On these two videos, Brad Leftwich teaches the fundamentals of
traditional "downbow" fiddling. His unique method helps players
learn how to produce the flowing, rhythmic sound that has delighted
square dancers and music lovers for generations. He also discusses
the use of tunings, drone strings, and double stops; simple variations; and, most importantly, bowing. Specific bow licks covered on
this tape are short and long saw-strokes, the shuffle, and beginning
and ending licks. (Homespun Tapes)

📖 *Old-Time Kentucky Fiddle Tunes* by Jeff Todd Titon

Biographical information on major players and transcriptions of 170
tunes, with a discography for each tune. Includes a CD containing
twenty-six performances that are notated in the book. (University
Press of Kentucky)

📼 *Southern Old-Time Fiddle Tour* with Bruce Molsky

On this instructional video, Molsky teaches six fiddle tunes from
this powerful musical tradition, each from a different geographi-
cal area and in a different tuning. For inspiration, Molsky draws
on historic recordings by pioneering artists such as Fiddlin' John
Carson, Carter Brothers and Son, Tommy Jarrell, Eck Robertson,
and Uncle Bunch Stevens. (Homespun Tapes)

💿 Supplemental Discography: Old-Time

Blizard, Ralph and the New Southern Ramblers, *Southern Ramble*
　　(Rounder)
Greene, Bruce, *Five Miles of Ellum Wood* (One Man Clapping)
Holcomb, Roscoe, *High Lonesome Sound* (Smithsonian Folkways)
Leftwich, Brad, *Say, Old Man* (County)
Poole, Charlie, *Old-Time Songs Recorded from 1925 to 1930* (County)
Robertson, Eck, *Old-time Texas Fiddling 1922–1929* (County)

Salyer, John, *Home Recordings 1941–1942* (The Appalachian Center at Berea College)

The Skillet Lickers, *Old-Time Fiddle Tunes and Songs from North Georgia* (County)

Taylor, Hollis, *Old Time Standards* (Twisted Fiddle)

Wine, Melvin, *Hannah at the Springhouse* (Arhoolie)

Anthology: *The Art of Old-Time Mountain Music* (Rounder)

Anthology: *Country Fiddle Classics* (County)

Anthology: *Echoes of the Ozarks, Volume 1 or 2* (County)

Anthology: *Fiddle Jam Session* (Voyager)

Bluegrass

Born in Kentucky in 1911, singer and mandolinist Bill Monroe has been credited as the founder of the bluegrass style. He was influenced by the Appalachian and "hillbilly" music that was popular with the farm families and blue-collar workers with whom he grew up, but he was equally influenced by the blues. The term *bluegrass* came from the Blue Grass Boys, the name of a band Monroe formed in 1934 that was popular in East Chicago and the Whiting, Indiana, area. The full sound of this genre took at least another ten years to formulate. Central to this evolution was the addition to the band of banjoist Earl Scruggs, who joined the band in late 1944.

The style itself has been fondly referred to by folklorist Alan Lomax as "folk music in overdrive." Known for its extreme tempos, a bluegrass band is made up of at least two singers (the vocal harmonies are fundamental to the style), banjo, mandolin, guitar, bass, and fiddle. Monroe introduced triple fiddles playing in three-part harmony in the 1950s, but most current bluegrass bands only have one fiddler. Some of the phenomenal fiddlers Monroe has worked with include Kenny Baker, Vassar Clements, Charlie Cline, Richard Greene, Bobby Hicks, Tex Logan, Joe Stuart, Red Taylor, and Gordon Terry.

There is a wonderful rhythmic counterpoint created between the instruments of a bluegrass band. The guitar generally carries the downbeat, while the other instruments create the "chop" or "chunk," consisting of a percussive stroke used to emphasize each upbeat. Fiddlers Richard Greene and Darol Anger have each developed chop technique on violin far beyond its original function. They can turn their fiddles into mini-percussion hubs.

Stylistic Characteristics

Bluegrass requires enormous technique from fiddlers. They must be able to play at extremely fast tempos, shift up and down the fingerboard, incorporate blue notes (flatted thirds and fifths) into the scale, and "take a break," meaning solo at the appropriate times.

Bluegrass slide technique includes a distinctive-sounding dip down out of the note, and its double-stops are more challenging than those of old-time fiddling. Rather than moving a melodic line against an open drone string, bluegrass double-stops tend to be fingered chords that place a harmony a third or sixth above or below the melodic line.

In addition to lightning-fast repetitive string crossings, chop technique—a percussive sound created when the bow drops vertically at the frog—is used to kick off tunes and support other soloists by emphasizing the second and fourth beats of the measure.

Artist Sampler

Vassar Clements (b. 1928)

Vassar Clements's phenomenal ability to play virtually any kind of music—from his own style, known as hillbilly jazz, to bluegrass, country, pop, rock, jazz, and swing—has garnered him five Grammy nominations. His performing and recording experience has been so diverse that his list of credits reads like a "who's who" of the music industry.

Clements has plied his bow with everyone from Earl Scruggs and Doc Watson to Chet Atkins, the Grateful Dead, B.B. King, Paul McCartney, the Monkees, Spinal Tap, the Boston Pops, John Sebastian, and Clarence Gatemouth Brown. At the age of fourteen, he debuted at the Grand Old Opry with Bill Monroe, and he toured with Monroe for fifteen years. His presence on the Nitty Gritty Dirt Band's 1972 crossover record *Will the Circle be Unbroken* introduced him to a younger pop audience. The classic record *Old & In the Way*, recorded live in 1973 with Jerry Garcia, Peter Rowan, David Grisman, and John Kahn, made him an instant favorite with fans of what has lately become known as jam band music (bands that feature improvisation, cross genre boundaries, and have a strong commitment to song craft). He has explored jazz with former Miles Davis band members Dave Holland, John Abercrombie, and Jimmy Cobb, and his collaboration with Stephane Grappelli earned him his fifth Grammy nomination.

🎧 Listen for

Beautifully constructed solos; comprehensive command of the fiddle; a distinctive voice on the instrument; able to relax back behind the beat in a calming manner while simultaneously spinning out well thought-out phrases at lightning tempos

Support Materials

📼 *The Fiddle According to Vassar* taught by Vassar Clements

On this video, the great fiddler Vassar Clements shows violinists and fiddlers how to apply blues and jazz influences to transform ordinary fiddle sounds into extraordinary ones. Players will have the opportunity to master more than a dozen of Clements's trademark licks, plus slides, chromatics, double and triple-stops, slurs, and boogie-woogie patterns. (Homespun Tapes)

61

🎵 Discography

Clements, Vassar, *Full Circle* (OMS)

Clements, Vassar, *Bottom Line Encore Collection* (Bottom Line/Koch)

Clements, Vassar, *Hillbilly Jazz* (Flying Fish)

Clements, Vassar with Jerry Garcia, *Old & In the Way* (Arista)

Richard Greene (b. 1942)

Richard Greene, in the words of the magazine *Bluegrass Unlimited*, is "one of the most innovative and influential fiddle players of all time." Growing up in Los Angeles, he dabbled in classical music until his encounter with the pyrotechnic fiddling of Scotty Stoneman permanently changed his musical direction. He first attained prominence with Bill Monroe and the Bluegrass Boys in 1966 as one of Monroe's first "Northern" band members. His advanced technique and intense yet "cool" tone amazed audiences and has influenced new generations of fiddle players.

In addition to founding the revolutionary folk-rock group Seatrain (in which he pioneered the electric violin in the rock genre), Greene has collaborated with some of the world's most talented musicians. These include the Jim Kweskin Jug Band, Clarence White (Muleskinner), Old & In the Way, the Blues Project, Gary Burton, Emmylou Harris, Tony Rice, Loggins & Messina, Peter Rowan, Rod Stewart, Jerry Garcia, Bruce Springsteen, Melissa Manchester, James Taylor, Dolly Parton, George Strait, Bob Seger, Andreas Vollenweider, Brian Wilson, Herbie Hancock, Van Dyke Parks, David Grisman, Crosby Stills & Nash, Buell Neidlinger, Deana Carter, Phish, Ice-T, and many others. Greene (with David Grisman in the Great American Music Band) is one of the undisputed inventors of "NewGrass" or "New Acoustic" instrumental music.

🎧 *Listen for*

Driving bow arm; impeccable intonation; well-crafted original solos and arrangements

Support Materials

📼 *Bluegrass Fiddle: A Private Lesson with Richard Greene*

This video teaches students essential bluegrass skills. These include warming up, producing good tone, tuning one's hand to one's instrument for proper intonation, and playing with "freedom and abandon." Greene presents a myriad of bluegrass bowing patterns and techniques: crossbowing, "separate" bowing, the bounced bow (spiccato), hemiola (accenting off beats), the "Georgia shuffle," and rhythm chopping. Greene also teaches double- and triple-stops; fingered unisons; the use of "bluesy" thirds, fifths, and sevenths; bluegrass slides; tricks for playing fast; and lessons on a handful of bluegrass tunes. (Homespun Tapes)

📖 *Richard Greene's Transcriptions*

This book presents transcriptions of the tunes contained on *The Grass Is Greener* CD. (Greener Grass Productions)

💿 *Discography*

Greene, Richard, *The Grass Is Greener* (Rebel)

Greene, Richard, *Greene Fiddler* (Sierra)

Greene, Richard, *Wolves A'Howling* (Rebel)

Greene, Richard, *Sales Tax Toddle* (Rebel)

Additional Support Materials: Bluegrass

📖 *Bluegrass Fiddle Styles* by Stacy Phillips and Kenny Kosek

This book features careful transcriptions of over sixty of the most influential bluegrass solos, along with analysis and historical background. Includes an accompanying cassette. (Music Sales Corp.)

🎵 *High and Lonesome: The Story of Bluegrass Music*

This DVD presents a historical picture of Monroe, the father of Kentucky bluegrass. A variety of bluegrass greats, including Flat and Scruggs, the Osborne Brothers, Jimmy Martin, and Alison Krauss, offer informative anecdotes, accompanied by evocative archival footage and concert performances from the bluegrass festival circuit. (Koch Vision/Shanachie)

📖 *Hot Licks for Bluegrass Fiddle* by Stacy Phillips

Over 450 authentic bluegrass licks are presented in this book, as well as information on how to apply them to create solo fills and backup. The book includes sections on double stops, upper positions, kickoffs, tags, fills, and a whole chapter on the ins and outs of the famous bluegrass tune "Orange Blossom Special." (Music Sales Corp.)

📼 *Learning Bluegrass Fiddle Pt. 1 and 2* with Kenny Kosek

Kenny Kosek's two videos on bluegrass and old-time country fiddle were created to get students jamming on their favorite tunes, even if they have never played a lick before. Kosek's phrase-by-phrase breakdowns make it easy to develop a strong repertoire of tunes. (Homespun Tapes)

📼 *The Orange Blossom Special* taught by Buddy Spicher

This video CD includes helpful chord charts and ideas to guide students through mastering this all-time fiddle tune favorite. It is a private lesson that plays on your personal computer. (Secter)

📖 *Teach Yourself Bluegrass Fiddle* by Matt Glaser

This book is intended for the beginning bluegrass fiddle player and contains a guide to technique, solos, backup, and achieving an authentic sound, as well as right- and left-handed playing. (Music Sales Corp.)

🎵 Supplemental Discography: Bluegrass

Duncan, Stuart, *Stuart Duncan* (Rounder Select)

Hicks, Bobby, *Texas Crapshooter* (County)

Hicks, Bobby, *Fiddle Patch* (Rounder)

Monroe, Bill, *The Music of Bill Monroe* [Box Set] (MCA)

Monroe, Bill, *Bill Monroe: All the Classic Releases 1937–1949* [Box Set] (JSP)

Spicher, Buddy, *Wildwood Flower* (Secter)

Spicher, Buddy, *In the Vernacular* (Secter)

Various artists, *The Bluegrass Album Band* (Rounder)

Cajun

In 1755, the British expelled the Acadians, the French settlers of the Maritime Provinces of Canada. A relatively small contingent of roughly 3,000 Acadians sailed to Louisiana between 1765 and 1785 to begin their lives anew. The fiddle came with them, as did a number of French, Scottish, and Irish tunes. The accordion and guitar, popular Cajun instruments today, didn't become a part of Cajun music until the 1900s.

Isolation, close family ties, and strong Catholic faith knit the Acadians into a tight cultural group whose style mixed with that of their close neighbors: Native Americans, Afro-Caribbean refugees from the West Indies, non-enslaved blacks, and various European immigrant groups. Isolated families had only themselves for entertainment, so most Acadians learned how to play musical instruments. Many made their own fiddles.

Stylistic Characteristics

Since the fiddle was central to community dances, fiddlers developed driving, rhythmic bow arms. Cajun fiddling uses long bows that drone the melody against open strings, a shuffle stroke bow pattern, and bluesy slides. Two fiddles are usually played together, one playing the lead melody and the other playing a rhythmic back-up called "bassing" or "seconding." Many tunes employ a triplet figure that loops back into an eighth-note motion and helps define the rhythmic signature of the music.

Fiddling legends of this style include Dewey Balfa, Harry Choates, Sady Courville, Michael Doucet, Wade Fruge, and Dennis McGee.

Artist Sampler

Dewey Balfa (1927–1992)

Dewey Balfa was born in Grand Louis, Louisiana, to Charles Balfa and Amay Ardoin. There was music in the Balfa household from the beginning, with Papa Charles playing the fiddle and singing ballads. By the age of ten, young Dewey had joined in. In the mid-1940s he formed the group the Musical Brothers and began playing at Hick's Wagonwheel Club. Along with his brothers, Will, Harry, Rodney, and Burkeman, Dewey began playing eight dances a week while holding down a full-time job.

In 1964, Balfa was called in as a last-minute replacement on guitar at the Newport Folk Festival. This was the first time Cajun music was to be featured in the national spotlight, and the idea of Cajun music representing Louisiana at such a prestigious event was more than a little disturbing to some. As Balfa described later, he had never played for more than two hundred people at once, and in Newport there were seventeen thousand—seventeen thousand people who, as it turned out, refused to let the musicians get off stage.

This incredible response was a major turning point for Balfa, who went home with a new sense of pride in his culture and his music. With his brothers, he formed the group the Balfa Brothers and began to tour internationally, in addition to maintaining his heartfelt involvement with music back home. Balfa continued performing until his death in 1992.

🎵 Listen for

Celebratory spirit; fluid, precise style; an abundance of heart and soul

💿 Discography

Balfa, Dewey, *Cajun Legend: Dewey Balfa* (Swallow)

Balfa, Dewey, *The Balfa Brothers Play Traditional Cajun Music* (Swallow)

Balfa, Dewey, *Under a Green Oak Tree* (Arhoolie)

Michael Doucet (b. 1951)

Growing up near Lafayette, Louisiana, at a time when the Cajun renaissance was just beginning, Michael Doucet did not fully appreciate the rich musical heritage of his native region until he visited France in 1973. His discovery there of French bands performing traditional Cajun music changed Doucet's life. On his return to Louisiana that same year, he sought out Cajun musicians Dewey Balfa, Canray Fontenot, and Dennis McGee. Through his ensuing friendship with McGee, Doucet learned about traditional Cajun music. The vibrant 1930s collaboration between Dennis McGee and Amédé Ardoin and their subsequent recordings had a particular impact on Doucet.

Doucet formed his band, Beausoleil, in the early 1970s. The group has gained international renown for its inspired interpretation of traditional Cajun music and its innovation in "Cajunizing" other musical styles: jazz, Caribbean, and even Tex-Mex.

🎵 Listen for

Textures smooth as wine but rough where needed; smoking ensemble playing; heartbreaking mood one minute, celebratory the next

Support Materials

📼 *Learn to Play Cajun Fiddle* taught by Michael Doucet

This video gives musicians the opportunity to add some Cajun classics to their set list. While learning to play over a dozen waltzes, two-steps, blues, and breakdowns, students will gain an understanding of the differences among Cajun, Creole, and zydeco styles. Doucet explains the stylistic devices—slurs, harmonies, and ornaments—that give this music its distinctive sound. (Homespun Tapes)

💿 Discography

Doucet, Michael, *Bayou Deluxe: The Best of Michael Doucet and Beausoleil* (Rhino)

Doucet, Michael, *Encore Encore the Best of Beausoleil 1991–2001* (Rhino)

Doucet, Michael, *Beau Solo* (Arhoolie)

Additional Support Materials: Cajun

💿 *J'ai Eté Au Bal* by Les Blank and Chris Strachwitz

This DVD presents an excellent overview of Cajun and zydeco music. (Brazos Films)

💿 Supplemental Discography: Cajun

Frugé, Wade, *Wade Frugé* (Arhoolie)

Frugé, Wade, *Old Style Cajun Music* (Arhoolie)

Kershaw, Doug, *The Best of Doug Kershaw* (Warner Brothers)

McGhee, Dennis, *En Bas Du Chene Vert* (Arhoolie)

McGhee, Dennis, *Cajun Legend* (Swallow)

Various artists, *Rough Guide: Cajun and Zydeco* (World Music Network)

Franco-American and Québécois

During the expulsion of French settlers from Canada's Maritime Provinces in the eighteenth century, thousands of Acadians escaped down through Canada to settle in the New England states, particularly Maine. They carried the same combination of Celtic and French musical traditions as their Acadian cousins who settled in Louisiana.

Stylistic Characteristics

In Franco-American music, the use of the bow is highly rhythmic, because it is the fiddle's job to tell the dancer's feet what to do. Players combine Irish-influenced ornamentation in the left hand with syncopation and off-beat accentuation in the right.

Artist Sampler

Louis Beaudoin (1921–1980)

In 1937, Louis Beaudoin's father moved his family to Burlington, Vermont, which would remain Beaudoin's home for the rest of his life. During World War II, Beaudoin served in Africa and Europe as a member of General Patton's tank corps. He joined the Northeast Fiddlers' Association when it was founded in 1966. He discovered that fellowship with other musicians inspired him to play. Beaudoin loved performing in public and played for many social occasions, as well as for the Vermont State Legislature, the Vermont Historical Society, and the Philadelphia Folk Festival.

ᯤ *Listen for*

Swinging, syncopated French rhythms; dancy, joyous energy; great ensemble work with brother Willie on guitar

ᯤ *Discography*

Beaudoin, Louis, *Louis Beaudoin* (Philo)

Donna Hébert (b. 1948)

A third-generation Franco-American and a daughter and granddaughter of New England millworkers, Donna Hébert is an important interpreter of the Franco-American style. A gifted songwriter as well, Hébert embodies French swing and syncopation in her interpretation of the music of her Québécois ancestors.

Her group, Chanterelle, plays the music of the French in America: the reels of New England, the songs and melodies of the Québécois and Franco-Americans, and the waltzes and two-steps of the Cajuns of Louisiana. Of particular note are Hébert's tireless efforts to document and teach Franco-American fiddle, both privately and in workshop.

🎧 Listen for

Fluid twists and turns; resonant tone; driving groove

Support Materials

📖 *The Grumbling Old Woman: Tunes for New England Contradancing* by Donna Hébert

A collection of Hébert's personal fiddling favorites—jigs, reels, marches, waltzes, and airs—tunes from Canada, the United States, and the British Isles, plus several originals, from one of the founders of the contradance renaissance. All tunes include chords and groove bowings. Also included are arrangements of Gilbert and Sullivan operettas for dancing. (Chanterelle)

💿 Discography

Hébert, Donna, *Kitchen Junket: Yankee Ingenuity* (Fretless)

Hébert, Donna, *Rude Awakening: Rude Girls* (Flying Fish)

Hébert, Donna, *French in America* (Chanterelle)

Hébert, Donna, *Soirée Chez Nous* (Chanterelle)

Western Swing

Texas represents the height of the cultural exchange we have examined in this book's discussion of American fiddle styles. Throughout the 1840s and 1850s, the migration West in search of gold and land drew fiddlers and other musicians from every region of the United States. Regional Mexican fiddle styles, string band music (see below), and African-American blues fiddle were combined with old-time music from the East to create a style unique to the Southwest. Country fiddling, cowboy songs, Big Band swing, and the blues/jazz tradition of improvisation all blended together in an acoustic string ensemble to produce Texas swing, also referred to as Western swing.

Two key musicians helped shape and popularize this style. Fiddler Bob Wills and vocalist Milton Brown began to perform together on Dallas radio in 1930. Originally called the Aladdin Laddies, they changed their name in honor of their 1931 sponsor to the Light Crust Doughboys. In 1932 each went on to lead his own band. Unfortunately, Milton Brown died in an automobile accident in 1936 and never received the exposure that Bob Wills enjoyed throughout his full career. Bob Wills and His Texas Playboys eventually swelled to include thirteen musicians, and later eighteen. Wills is fondly referred to as the "King of Western Swing."

Fiddlers of particular note in this style include Jesse Ashlock, Keith Coleman, Spade Cooley, Johnny Gimble, Joe Holley, Dale Potter, Buddy Spicher, Louis Tierney, and Vassar Clements.

Stylistic Characteristics

Texas-style fiddling is distinguished by its smooth melodic phrasing, which is produced by a combination of complex fingering and long bow strokes. The style uses syncopation and adds left-hand ornamentation to the melody. The Texas-style fiddler improvises variations on the melodic line after performing the melody. He or she also plays short improvised fills between the vocal lines or prearranged riffs punctuating the melody.

Most of the Western swing repertoire is based around songs rather than instrumentals, but the fiddle still plays a central role in its arrangements. The melodies are often led by the fiddles— usually twin fiddles playing in harmony, emphasizing the third or sixth above or below the melody. Some bands are comprised of larger fiddle sections playing in unison or harmony.

Artist Sampler
Dale Potter (1929–1996)

Originally from southeast Missouri, Dale Potter played the mandolin before switching to fiddle as his primary instrument. Probably best known for his fabulous double-stop fiddle work, Potter grew up listening to Bob Wills on the radio and, as a youth, mistook the Texas Playboys' twin fiddles for the work of a single musician. In an effort to emulate that sound, Potter developed an astonishing facility for self-harmonizing via the use of double-stops.

⑨ *Listen for*
Amazing harmonies that flow like oil; high-spirited solos

💿 *Discography*
Potter, Dale, *Country Waltz Time* (Stoneway)
Potter, Dale, *Hoe Down, Vol. 1 Rural Rhythm* (RRDP)
Potter, Dale, *Super Fiddle* (Stoneway)
Potter, Dale, *Unique Fiddle Style of Dale Potter* (Stoneway)

Johnny Gimble (b. 1926)

Born in the east Texas town of Tyler, Gimble and his four brothers grew up on a one-hundred-acre farm. Gimble reports that his older brother Jack was the first to pick up an instrument. Eventually, they all began to play. Gimble started playing the fiddle when he was nine.

His first break came in 1949 when a band he was playing in called the Rhythmaires opened for Bob Wills and His Texas Playboys. Jesse Ashlock, Wills's fiddle player at the time, had just given notice, so the band invited Gimble to join them. Gimble played with the Playboys for most of the 1950s.

In 1961, Gimble became fiddler for *Five Star Jubilee,* a show broadcast on NBC from Springfield, Missouri. Following a brief layoff from the music business in the mid-sixties, he moved to Nashville and became the most in-demand fiddle player in the region for the next decade.

Gimble has recorded with Asleep at the Wheel, Chet Atkins, Joan Baez, Jimmy Buffett, Guy Clark, Jessi Colter, the Everly Brothers, Merle Haggard, Waylon Jennings, Loretta Lynn, Paul McCartney & Wings, Reba McEntire, Tracy Nelson and Mother Earth, Willie Nelson, Dolly Parton, Pure Prairie League, Leon Russell, Connie Smith, Conway Twitty, Porter Wagoner, and too many others to list.

In 1975, and for four consecutive years after that, Gimble was named the Country Music Association's Instrumentalist of the Year. He was also named Fiddler of the Year nine times by the Academy of Country Music.

In the late 1970s Gimble moved back to his home state, Texas.

ʒ Listen for

Fiery melodic solos; infectious enthusiasm; the matching of precision with Texas soul

Discography

Gimble, Johnny, *The Texas Fiddle Collection: Johnny Gimble* (CMH)

Gimble, Johnny, *Texas Honky-Tonk Hits: Johnny Gimble* (CMH)

Additional Support Materials: Western Swing

Western Swing Fiddle by Stacy Phillips

This book includes over one hundred transcriptions of classic swing fiddle solos from 1928 to the present with discography, bibliography, and rare photos. (Oak Publications)

🎵 Supplemental Discography: Western Swing

Anastasio, Paul, *Twin Fiddle Western Swing* (Swing Cat Enterprises)

Brown, Milton, *Milton Brown and his Musical Brownies* Box Set (Proper Box)

Spicher, Buddy, *Western Swing* (Secter)

Wills, Bob, *Bob Wills & His Texas Playboys: For the Last Time* (Capitol)

Wills, Bob, *Papa's Jumpin'* (Bear Family)

Wills, Bob, *The Essential Bob Wills & His Texas Playboys* (Sony)

Wills, Bob, *Take Me Back to Tulsa* [Box Set] (Proper Box)

Wills, Bob, *The King of Western Swing: 25 Hits 1935–1945* (ASV Living Era)

Various artists, *Heroes of Country Music Vol. 1 Legends of Western Swing* (Rhino)

Various artists (including the legendary Benny Thomasson), *Texas Fiddle Bands* (Arhoolie)

String Bands

In the late 1800s and early 1900s, string bands were the South's most popular form of entertainment. The fiddle most often shared leadership with the vocalist, playing the main melodic line in an unornamented style and then continuing behind the singer. The black string band tradition, which began before the American Revolution and continued into the early 1930s, included a good deal of fiddle improvisation.

Early American string bands performed throughout the South at picnics, square dances, Saturday night parties, and family and social gatherings. The original bands consisted of fiddle, banjo (originally *banjar*, an instrument from Africa), guitar, and later, mandolin.

Most early groups had an eclectic repertoire: they played country dance tunes, and, later, blues, ragtime numbers, popular songs, and jazz. Few of these musicians had formal training of any kind, and their tradition was aural. Never lacking in spirit, however, musicians such as black fiddler Chasey Collins played with such gusto that their rusty sound could easily be forgiven.

Some groups that were popular in the early thirties could play in any key and had vast repertoires of original as well as popular folk and blues tunes. One of these groups, the Tennessee Chocolate Drops, was made up of mandolinist Carl Martin, guitarist Ted Bogan, and fiddler Howard Armstrong. After their rise to fame in the 1930s, the Tennessee Chocolate Drops disappeared from the music scene for many years. Later, in the 1960s, they re-emerged as Martin, Bogan, and Armstrong, gaining national popularity on the folk music scene.

Popular groups such as the Mississippi Sheiks placed the fiddle in a central position, and for good reason: fiddlers such as Lonnie Chatmon had a solid command of the instrument. In fact, under the guiding influence of Chatmon, the Mississippi Sheiks became one of the few professional string bands in the Mississippi area. They performed for white audiences more than black, and, according to brother Sam Chatmon, Lonnie pursued music as a livelihood because he didn't like farming and "I was tired of smelling mule farts"! The Mississippi Sheiks recorded roughly seventy-five sides in the late twenties and early thirties, as well as dozens of others using pseudonyms such as the Mississippi Mud Steppers and the Mississippi Hot Footers to get around the limitations of their record contract.

🎵 Discography

Barnyard Dance: Martin, Bogan, and Armstrong (Rounder)

Black Fiddlers (Document)

Folks, He Sure Do Pull Some Bow! 1927–1935 (Old Hat)

Jug, Jook, and Washboard Bands (Arhoolie)

Low Down Memphis Barrelhouse Blues (Mamlish)

Rural String Bands of Tennessee (County)

Stop and Listen: The Mississippi Sheiks (Mamlish)

Strings Bands 1926–1929 (Document)

Additional Support Materials: American Fiddle

📼 *A Fiddler's Guide to Waltzes, Aires, and Haunting Melodies* taught by Jay Ungar

This video teaches students to play lovely, heart-rending pieces, benefiting from Jay Ungar's years of experience as a top fiddler. Ungar shows the inventive use of slides, grace notes, rolls, smears, vibrato, and special bowing techniques that turn ordinary tunes into distinctive compositions. He teaches "Tombigbee Waltz," "Tennessee Waltz," "South Wind," "Shebeg Shemor," "Give Me Your Hand" and his Grammy-winning "Ashokan Farewell." (Homespun Tapes)

📖 *Barrage, Volume I and Volume II* written and arranged by Dean Marshall

The Barrage volumes combine jazz, swing, Celtic roots, rock, klezmer, country, calypso, and every musical style in between. The companion enhanced CD has two exciting applications. The piano/guitar accompaniment sheet music can be printed from a computer, and the same CD can be inserted in a stereo for play along with the pre-recorded piano accompaniment tracks. (Mel Bay Publications)

📖 *The Complete Country Fiddler* by Stacy Phillips

Authentic licks, three hundred solos, interviews with top professional players, and a discussion of fiddle amplification are featured in this book. Includes a companion cassette. (Mel Bay Publications)

📖 *The Fiddle Book* by Marion Thede

This book features over 150 tunes, familiar and obscure, with lyrics and cross-tuning systems. (Music Sales Corp.)

📖 *The Fiddler's Fakebook* by David Brody

Nearly five hundred tunes from all the major fiddling traditions are contained in this book. (Music Sales Corp.)

📖 Fiddler Magazine's *Favorites*

Fiddler Magazine, in conjunction with Mel Bay Publications, has compiled a wonderful collection of tunes and interviews with contributions from thirty-six of the world's greatest fiddlers. Featured artists are Charlie Acuff, Paul Anastasio, Randal Bays, Byron Berline, Kevin Burke, Vassar Clements, Michael Doucet, Jackie Dunn, J.P. Fraley, Johnny Gimble, Bruce Greene, John Hartford, Richard Greene, Ivan Hicks, Jerry Holland, Olav Johansson, James Kelly, Barbara Lamb, Laurie Lewis, Sandy MacIntyre, Natalie MacMaster, Frankie McWhorter, Bruce Molsky, Juan Reynoso, Dale Russ, Oliver Schorer, Pierre Schryer, Bjorn Stabi, Alicia Svigals, Athena Tergis, & Laura Risk, Jay Ungar, Jean-Marie Verret, Claude Williams, George Wilson, and Jennifer Wrigley. (Mel Bay Publications)

📖 *Fiddlers Philharmonic* by Andrew Dabczynski and Bob Phillips

This popular series of books encourages fun, skill-building fiddling on all string instruments. Each fiddle tune is presented as a solo in a common key to facilitate group playing. Includes accompaniment and practice CDs and a teacher's manual. (Alfred Publications)

📖 *Fiddle Solos*

Mel Bay's *Anthology of Fiddle Solos* is designed to enhance the repertoire of the intermediate to advanced fiddler. This generous collection of challenging pieces by many leading composers, arrangers, performers, and teachers includes some of the best tunes by Paul Anastasio, Peter Anick, Byron Berline, Robin Bullock, Vassar Clements, Peter Cooper, Frank Ferrel, Martin Hayes, Jerry Holland, Kenny Kosek, Natalie MacMaster, Stacy Phillips, Jay Ungar, and many others. (Mel Bay Publications)

📖 *The Fiddle Club* by Dean Marshall and John Crozman

These three books feature unique collections of traditional and original folk tunes. Available with guitar/piano accompaniment on CD or as demonstrated by the Calgary Fiddlers. (Mel Bay Publications)

📖 *Fiddling Around the World* by Chris Haigh

This book describes fourteen fiddle styles from around the world and offers forty-eight original and traditional tunes to illustrate the styles. A bibliography of recordings and books relevant to each style is included. (Spartan Press)

📼 *Mark O'Connor's Fiddle Camp* taught by Mark O'Connor

Take a center seat in Mark O'Connor's exciting "Back To Basics" class (filmed at his popular annual Fiddle Camp). O'Connor points out items of stylistic and technical importance and helps students develop their ears. Students will master a wide variety of basic fiddle techniques and learn to play three tunes in phrase-by-phrase detail by the end of this easy-going, play-along session. (Homespun Tapes)

📖 *Mark O'Connor: The Championship Years* by Stacy Phillips

Written with O'Connor's help, this book includes meticulous transcriptions of O'Connor's trend-setting performances at fiddle contests. Interviews and detailed analysis are included. (Mel Bay Publications)

📖 *Ryan's Mammoth Collection of Fiddle Tunes* edited by Patrick Sky

This comprehensive book is a facsimile edition of the original collection published in 1883. It has survived over the years because it is one of the richest and most interesting of the nineteenth-century instrumental collections, as well as a resource for students of American vernacular music. (Mel Bay Publications)

💿 Supplemental Discography: American Fiddle

Hartford, John, *The Speed of the Bow* (Rounder)
Kosek, Kenny, *Angelwood* (Rounder Select)
Ungar, Jay, *The Lover's Waltz* (Angel)
Ungar, Jay, *Harvest Home* (Angel)
Waller, Julianna, with Cowboy Joe Baer, *Daybreak* (d'Note)

Compilations

American Fiddle Tunes, featuring twenty-seven tracks from fiddlers
throughout America (Rounder)

Diary of a Fiddler, featuring Darol Anger, Natalie MacMaster,
Vassar Clements, Stuart Duncan, and Martin Hayes (Compass)

Fiddlers Four, with Darol Anger, Bruce Molsky, Michael Doucet,
and Rushad Eggleston (Compass)

Heroes, featuring Mark O'Connor with Jean-Luc Ponty, Stephane
Grappelli, Pinchas Zukerman, L. Shankar, Byron Berline,
Kenny Baker, Vassar Clements, Benny Thomasson, Terry Morris,
Texas Shorty, Doug Kershaw, Johnny Gimble, Charlie Daniels,
and Buddy Spicher (Warner Brothers)

Masters of Folk Violin, with Brendan Mulvihill, Kenny Baker, Claude Williams,
Michael Doucet, and Natalie MacMaster (Arhoolie)

American String Teachers Association
National Conference
March 2003

Jesus Florido, Mark Wood,
and Julie Lyonn Lieberman

Bruce Molsky, Leanne Darling,
and Vicki Richards

Top row, left to right: Matt Glaser, Bruce Molsky,
Robert Gardner, Liz Carroll, Leanne Darling,
Julie Lyonn Lieberman, Mark Wood,
Paul Anastasio, and Jesus Florido

Bottom row, left to right: Stanley Chepaitis,
Christian Howes, Vicki Richards, and
Renata Bratt

Strings in Blues and Jazz   5

Historic Overview: Blues Fiddle

The inception of slavery in the United States inadvertently triggered a major shift in the role the violin would play in American music. The popular styles of string music up until that time had consisted of imported traditions, such as classical and Celtic (Irish, English, and Scottish). In the early days of slavery, many plantation owners taught their slaves how to fiddle and play classical repertoire to entertain at family social functions. They even rented their slaves out to play at square dances and balls. Excellence on the fiddle provided a slightly gentler life for the slave than that of a field hand. Slaves taught to play both fiddle and classical violin adapted the instrument to mirror their vocal music, and, as the blues style evolved, the violin was central to this new art form.

It is not surprising that voice and violin were the earliest instruments involved in playing the blues. Both can slide in and out of pitch, tumble effortlessly through semi-tones, and tease and tickle the ears—howling one moment and whispering the next.

Over two hundred years later, the recording industry emerged in time to catch the tail end of the blues fiddle tradition. By the early 1930s, there were over fifty recorded blues fiddlers. However, we can assume that there were—and had been— many more. Almost all of the blues fiddlers that recorded did so between 1924 and 1931. Only a handful of players, such as Henry Son Sims, Carl Martin, Howard Armstrong, and Butch

Due to a resurgence of interest in folk music in the 1960s and '-70s, Howard Armstrong, as well as the left-handed blues fiddler Butch Cage, had a "second chance" to bring the art of blues fiddling to the public's attention. There were also a few records released at that time by labels such as Arhoolie and Mamlish (and later by Old Hat), which included re-releases of some of the early blues fiddlers.

Cage, fiddled the country blues into later decades.

Due to racism, blacks could not record on the same label as whites. Okeh Records (later to become Columbia) was the first record company to create a separate label for blacks, called Race Records. Along with Clifford Hayes, Lonnie Johnson and his brother James "Steady Roll" were among the first of the black blues fiddlers that Okeh recorded. Because 78-rpm records only allowed for slightly over three minutes of music per side, most groups developed a standard arrangement to fit into that time. Blues singers using fiddle tended to open their songs with a fiddle intro, sing a verse or two, segue into a fiddle solo, go back to a few more sung verses, and then close with a tag, which was usually played by the fiddler. Nap Hayes, who recorded *Violin Blues* with T.C. Johnson in 1928, is one of the only early recorded examples of a blues fiddler using the violin as a featured solo instrument.

Most of the blues fiddlers who were recorded, such as Will Batts, Lonnie Johnson, and Charlie Pierce, played fiddle tunes in addition to accompanying blues vocalists. Living in Georgia, Mississippi, and other rural areas throughout the South, blues fiddlers also played in string bands and had to be versatile in popular styles in addition to the blues. They had to know scores of tunes to entertain segregated white and black audiences.

A number of the primary blues fiddlers of the early 1900s migrated north to the cities, where they found work playing for silent films. In an interview for my National Public Radio series *The Talking Violin*, jazz bassist Milt Hinton mentioned that most of these fiddlers earned enough to buy their own houses in cities such as Chicago. With the arrival of the talking film and the development of large, noisy bars (the violin could not compete with horns or drums, and amplification did not yet exist), many blues fiddlers had to turn to rolling cigars for a living, while others survived by playing nights in local bordellos.

During the early 1930s, the blues fiddle tradition began to fade away. During that same time period, a handful of jazz violinists surfaced, such as Eddie South, Juice Wilson, Joe Venuti, and, in France, Stephane Grappelli. We do not really know why a whole generation of blues fiddlers did not make the transition into jazz. The new violinists emerged with greatly superior technique and harmonic expertise, playing swing music. Blues tunes were included in their repertoire but with a completely new level of harmonic and technical complexity. While this group of jazz violinists did not reflect the homespun, raw expressiveness of the early players, you can hear aspects of the blues fiddlers' style in certain techniques they established on the instrument.

Before blues fiddle, we have no evidence of slide technique or the bending of notes on the instrument. Because in the early development of the blues, the sound of the violin mimicked that of the voice, we can probably assume that players translated vocal techniques from Africa onto the instrument and carried these sounds into jazz violin. Syncopated figures and textural ideas were also carried forward.

Historic Overview: Jazz Violin

With the invention of pickups in the early 1940s and the advent of the use of mikes and amps in clubs, violins began to figure more prominently in clubs and Big Bands. The best-known jazz violinists were American players Joe Venuti, Eddie South, and Stuff Smith, as well as European-born Stephane Grappelli and Svend Asmussen. Unlike their blues fiddle predecessors, these musicians often led their own bands and, in some cases, composed their own original material.

In the forties and fifties, black jazz violinists such as Eddie South and Stuff Smith had to contend with racial discrimination. They were received well in Europe, but in America they were often confined to playing smaller clubs for very little money. Eddie

South's white friend and professional equal, Joe Venuti, could play all the classy establishments. There was one occasion when Venuti convinced a Big Band to hire South as a substitute, but they agreed only under the condition that he play behind a screen! A black jazz violinist could not even turn to the classical field to earn a better living in those days. Jazz violinist Joe Kennedy, Jr., once told me that the conductor of the Virginia Symphony Orchestra felt that Joe would have been chosen as concertmaster had he not been black. In fact, he was denied a seat in the orchestra altogether. Despite these conditions, South and Smith both enjoyed faithful, enthusiastic audiences.

Few of the Big Bands used full string sections, so the violinist functioned as a guest soloist. In some cases, horn players, like Ray Nance (trumpet) and Ray Perry (alto sax), doubled on violin. At the start of his career in the 1930s, jazz violinist Claude Williams was primarily a jazz guitarist in the Count Basie band. Almost all of the Big Bands were comprised mostly of horns supported by a rhythm section.

Blues Versus Jazz

The blues form is built over twelve bars. It can consist of as few as three chords (country blues) or, in the more complex jazz blues form, one chord per measure. Jazz standards are usually built over a thirty-two bar form consisting of an AABA format (each section eight bars in length) and utilize far more chords than blues in their harmonic motion. "Rhythm Changes," a popular thirty-two bar form, is a relatively simple entrée into extended jazz form, as the player can begin by improvising in one key, except on the bridge (B section).

Why Add Blues and Jazz to Your Curriculum?

Blues and jazz are America's classical music. Originally a product of the African-American experience in America, they have evolved to become a national and international expression, simultaneously influencing and being influenced by the music of the entire world. Jazz pianist and educator Billy Taylor aptly describes jazz as "a musical language that articulates authentic American feelings and thoughts."

Just as Bach built his compositions from playful improvisations, jazz continuously generates informal improvisations that become crystallized into repeatable forms, thereby renewing itself and evolving. It is a living art, and one that your students should be exposed to. After all, if we lived in France and were teaching the culinary arts, would we ignore the use of French spices and sauces? Would we serve only pizza because one group of people decided that it was the only food worth eating?

Sheet Music for Blues and Jazz

Just as classical music has defined a standard repertoire consisting of concertos, partitas, sonatas, symphonic works, and so forth, so has jazz. This repertoire consists of "jazz standards," which include thirty-two bar swing tunes, bossa novas, twelve-bar blues tunes, and select tunes by more contemporary jazz composers such as Thelonius Monk and Paquito D'Rivera. While the melodies are often technically simple, the improvisations generated by the soloist can become quite complex. Once the artist performs the melody, he or she goes on to use the scales generated by the chord symbols as a basis for the improvised melodic lines that comprise the solo. This requires knowledge of and facility in all twelve keys over seven basic chord types—and therefore seven basic chordal scales.

There are also composed blues and jazz arrangements for string orchestra. While limited in number, more are being generated every year. In fact, an ad hoc twenty-seven-member string group, comprised of players including Darol Anger, John Blake, Jr., Renata Bratt, Christian Howes, Matt Glaser, Joe Deninzon, Tanya Kalmanovitch, Martin Norgaard, and myself, premiered ten Bert Ligon jazz string charts for orchestra at the 2001 International Association of Jazz Educators conference to

Renata Bratt, Darol Anger, David Baker, and Martin Norgaard at the 2003 IAJE Conference

a standing ovation, and again at the 2003 American String Teacher Conference. These charts are available through StringsCentral.com and can provide your students with a taste of the blues, Latin, and jazz styles. It is also important to spend time teaching students how to improvise within those styles in order to be authentic to the genre.

Preparation for the Jazz Band

Every jazz musician, regardless of his or her instrument, must learn jazz chords, scales and modes, patterns, and repertoire. Then comes the struggle to integrate all of that information and technique into his or her own personal soloistic voice on that instrument.

For bowed string instruments, all of this effort is pointless without proper amplification. In order to solo over a whole band or orchestra, your students will need some kind of sound reinforcement, even if only from a microphone that they step up to for their solos.

Intonation is often problematic when a string player joins a traditional jazz band setting (consisting of horns, drums, piano, and bass). This is because it can be difficult to hear one's instrument in such a large band context. Coach your students to position their amps or monitors such that they are tilted up towards their ears. If budget permits, players can also invest in ear buds. Placed in the ears, these can both boost the sound of the player's instrument and mute the other instruments to some extent.

Proper band etiquette consists of understanding the band's expectations of the soloist—and the soloist's of the band. The melodic instruments will perform the "head" of the tune (the composed melody); trade solos on the chord changes, which can consist of anywhere from one to more than three "choruses" per soloist (each chorus comprised of the complete twelve- or thirty-two bar form); trade "fours" with the other band members (consisting of four bars each, across at least one chorus); and return to the head.

Stylistic Characteristics: The Blues

All styles require faithfulness to the characteristics that define them. Therefore, mastery of any style requires learning how to coordinate one's hands to phrase in a very specific manner. In the case of the blues, notes are not always sounded out straight-on. The player often slides or bends into (or out of) pitch, varying the length and speed of his or her slide. The blues is an art form that encompasses juicy, heartfelt melodies intertwined with soulful, gutsy solos. A uniquely American tradition, it calls upon the player's expressivity. There is a tempestuous relationship between the bow and the string rather than the even-pressured tendency of the classical genre. The blues scales used are often pentatonic (five-note), always adorned by a flatted seventh, and hungrily open to the possibility of a flatted third or fifth. The player must repeat these scales enough times to register them into both muscle memory and a mental image so that, when it comes time to improvise, the necessary pathways on the fingerboard are readily available, much like a map.

Stylistic Characteristics: Jazz

To convert from classical tonality and technique to jazz, there are several important issues that must be addressed. Primary among these are mastering the ability to play in flat keys, developing a chromatic motion on the fingerboard, learning to play with and without vibrato (see below), becoming comfortable with syncopated rhythms, and developing a working knowledge of chord changes.

Chromatic motion and flat keys, often used in jazz, require dividing first position into three positions: half position, first, and extended. Teach your students to practice leaning the hand back at an angle (bringing the left elbow forward and in) to access flatted notes such as the Db (on viola and cello), Ab, Eb, Bb, and F natural (on violin) played by the first finger just above the nut. For third-finger notes such as F# (on viola and cello), C#, G#, D#, and A# (on violin), students can relax their thumbs and allow the frames of their hands to shift a half step higher, although technically keeping their thumbs in first position.

Jazz vibrato has a wide range of sounds, from slow and wide; to a rolling classical sound; to a fast, wide, "hysterical" quality. Vibrato should always be practiced by rolling under and then up to pitch. Set a metronome at sixty and ask students to place their second fingers on a note high enough on the fingerboard

Regina Carter

that their hands are free of the scroll. Have students start with a quarter-note roll, hitting the targeted pitch on the tick and rolling slightly under the pitch on the next tick, then back again on the tick after that. Suggest that students aim when rolling to create "smile lines" across their fingers. Then have them roll using eighth-notes, triplets, and, finally, sixteenths. The faster the rhythm, the narrower the roll will need to be. This exercise will enable students to develop control over width and speed, the two elements that define vibrato. Instruct students to maintain a light touch while practicing the rolls. For wide, "hysterical" vibrato, students will need to skate on top of the string, using a fast motion back and forth that is powered by the forearm.

One of the distinct differences between a classical sound and a jazz sound on a bowed stringed instrument is created through left- and right-hand pressure. In classical music, the bow's movement on the string remains rather symmetrical and even, as does the left-hand. In jazz, this pressure must be varied. Tell students to imagine that the strings are trampolines, and ask them to practice lightly bouncing each finger up and down on random pitches. This will enable them to explore a range of pressures, from pressing down lightly onto the fingerboard to resting the fingertip on the surface of the string. Next, allow students' bow hands to mimic the up-and-down motion generated by the fingers of their left hands. Finally, challenge students to play a scale using quick, light bounces of the left-hand fingers, never firmly touching the fingerboard, while allowing the bow-hand to mirror this motion. This exercise will help students create what we call "ghost notes" in jazz violin technique: melodic notes that are implied lightly rather than sounded out fully.

To help students break away from symmetrical classical bowings, challenge them to play a melody with continuous upbows. Help them activate a swing sound by slurring continuous eighth-notes on a scale from the upbeat to the downbeat.

Notes in jazz are colored closely to the expressions of the human voice. Challenge your students to listen to their own voices when they sigh, moan, groan, or whoop with enthusiasm. Then ask them to try to match those sounds on their instruments as a warm-up to working on slides and bends.

There are three parameters to experiment with when sliding up into a note or down out of it: the speed of the slide, the distance, and the degree of pressure on the string. Beginners tend to favor one type of slide and continually use it the same way, often on the downbeat opening each phrase. Watch out for this, and coach your students. Make sure they practice sliding into notes on upbeats within the phrase as well. Ask them to practice varying their slides as much as possible.

A bend is created by placing the finger directly on top of the note, then rolling it under pitch, and finally rolling back up to pitch. Unlike the slide, the bend does not require the finger to glide on the surface of the string. Instead, it tilts.

Historically speaking, the violin's sound in jazz has ranged from a coarse, gutsy quality created by playing with hard staccato landings at the frog (Stuff Smith) to a singing tone generated by sweeping the bow (Stephane Grappelli). Jazz violinists generally use shorter bows rather than the classical sweeping bow and use vibrato only as a "seasoning" rather than the "main course." Slides in and out of notes, chromatic passing tones, and ghost notes are all colorations that help create the jazz sound. Rather than attacking notes in the symmetrical, crisp fashion characteristic of classical music, the syncopated use of the bowing arm, coupled with a left-hand slide technique, can create an effect that is more like a snake ambling and slithering its way along.

As with any style that you teach, jazz involves a new language that is best strengthened through listening. In addition to working on the above techniques, it is important to expose your students to recordings as much as possible and even challenge them to jam with these recordings.

Artist Sampler: Blues Fiddle

Will Batts (1904–1956)

Will Batts was considered one of the best blues fiddlers in the Memphis area. During the 1920s and '30s, he played with Jack Kelly, Dan Sane, Frank Stokes, and D.M. Higgs in a group called the South Memphis Jug Band. One of the longest surviving jug bands, the group was originally called Jack Kelly's Jug Busters.

Batts recorded thirteen sides with his jug band between 1929 and 1933. He also used the pseudonym "Bast" to record other sessions outside the group.

Lonnie Chatmon (1890s–1942 or 1943)

The Chatmon family came from Mississippi. Lonnie was one of eleven brothers and one sister, and all of the Chatmon children learned how to play instruments at an early age. Individually and collectively, the Chatmons (including half-brother Walter Vincson) recorded well over 150 record sides, 104 of which included either Lonnie or his brother Bo on fiddle. As performers, the Chatmon family was mainly known as the group the Mississippi Sheiks, but they also recorded under numerous pseudonyms.

Lonnie Johnson (1889–1970)

Lonnie Johnson was born Alonzo Johnson to a New Orleans family of eleven musical sisters and one brother. Between 1914 and 1917, Johnson played violin in his father's band in Storyville brothels and clubs. In 1917, while in England entertaining the troops, he lost most of his family back home to an influenza epidemic.

Johnson had a long and productive career. He played violin, guitar, bass, mandolin, and banjo, and he sang. He played violin in the Charlie Creath Band before forming his own group, featuring Deloise Searcy on piano and Johnson's brother James on guitar and violin. Lonnie Johnson died in Toronto in 1970 after a serious car accident.

Support Materials: Blues Fiddle

📼 *Blues on the Fiddle* by Darol Anger

Using a "call and response" interactive learning method, students can trade licks with Anger as they learn tunes, riffs, and styles from the Mississippi Delta to blues-inflected bluegrass, bebop, jazz, and even rock and roll. On this video, Anger analyzes the pentatonic (five-note) blues scale and its added "blue notes" and teaches how you can easily transpose licks and tunes from one key to another. By using the right vibrato, bowing techniques, intonation, and other nuances, it won't be long before students are riffing and jamming in all the blues styles. (Homespun Tapes)

📖 *Rockin' Out with Blues Fiddle* by Julie Lyonn Lieberman

This comprehensive guide to playing the blues on bowed strings is complete with warm-ups, patterns, pentatonic scales, tunes, and historical information. Includes a practice CD. (Huiksi Music)

💿 Discography: Blues Fiddle

Armstrong, Howard *Louie Bluie* (Arhoolie)

Cage, Butch, Willie B. Thomas, and others, *Country Negro Jam Session* (Arhoolie)

Hardy, Heather, *Violins* (Mush)

Folks, He Sure Do Pull Some Bow! African-American Fiddlers 1927–1935 (Old Hat)

Violin, Sing the Blues for Me: African-American Fiddlers 1926–1949 (Old Hat)

Artist Sampler: Jazz Violin

Eddie South (1904–1962)

Eddie South (Edward Otha South) was born in Louisiana, Missouri. He attended school in Chicago and started studying the violin with Charlie Elgar when he was ten years old. At sixteen, he went on to study at the Chicago College of Music with Petrowitsch Bissing. His early professional engagements included performances with Charlie Elgar's band, work as the musical director of Jimmie Wade's Syncopators, and a short stint with Erskine Tate and his orchestra. In 1928, a tour with Marian Harris took him to Europe. Even though the tour fell apart, it served an important purpose: South's introduction to Europe opened educational and professional doors that were not available to a man of color in America.

South stayed in Europe long enough to study with Firman Touche at the Paris Conservatory, as well as with Gypsy violinist Jazoz Derzo at the Budapest Conservatory. He also recorded with guitarist Django Reinhardt and jazz violinist Stephane Grappelli in 1937 in Paris, shortly before returning to the United States. South played some radio gigs in the 1940s and a television show in the 1950s. However, for the most part, his dark skin forced him to settle for nightclubs and second-rate theaters, even though he was fully capable of a sparkling concert career.

⑨ Listen for

Fine classical training; Gypsy-like rhapsodizing; driving, swinging use of the bow; a warm, lyrical sound

💿 Discography

South, Eddie, *Eddie South: Black Gipsy* (Epm Musique)

South, Eddie, *Solo, Trio and Orchestra, Broadcasts, Film and Fugitive, 1940-1947* (AB Fable)

Hezekiah Leroy Gordon Stuff Smith (1909–1967)

Stuff Smith was born in Portsmouth, Ohio. His first major professional engagement was with the Aunt Jemima Review, followed by the Alphonso Trent Orchestra—both in the 1920s. He had a brief two-week stint with Jelly Roll Morton, only to return to Trent.

In the mid-1930s, Smith began performing under his own name at the Onyx Club in New York City. His solo career took him to Europe in 1957 and then again in 1965, at which point he stayed for good. His recordings with a wide range of artists—including jazz violinist Stephane Grappelli, jazz trumpeter Dizzy Gillespie, and concert pianist Robert Crum—demonstrate his equally wide range of abilities as an artist, as well as his unmistakable sound. Smith died in Munich in 1967.

⑨ *Listen for*

Advanced harmonic explorations; quintessential swing; intense, exciting rhythms; chromatic patterns; emotional playing; textures from rough to sweet

❸ *Discography*

Smith, Stuff, *Complete Verve Stuff Smith Sessions* (Mosaic)

Smith, Stuff, *Stuff Smith 1944–1946: Studio, Broadcast, Concert and Apartment Performances* (AB Fable)

Smith, Stuff, (with Asmussen, Grappelli, and Ponty) *Violin Summit* (MPS)

Joe Venuti (1903–1978)

Joe Venuti's career spanned six decades and included over two dozen recordings. He started performing in the early 1920s, and it was obvious from his first recording in 1926 that he had a highly developed jazz violin sound. One of Venuti's earliest collaborations was with jazz guitarist Eddie Lang, which lasted twelve years, until Lang's premature death in 1933. After Lang's death, Venuti performed with a number of different guitarists, Big Bands, and various ensembles before he began touring under his own name.

Always reaching for perfection as a violinist and a jazz musician, Venuti was unique in that he collaborated with many different jazz artists in his constant exploration of the instrument and the art form. He even invented a new bow technique early in his career. He took the pin out of the end of his bow, placed the hair across all four strings, and played beautifully thought-out three- and four-note chords. This technique can be heard in his 1975 recording of "C-Jam Blues" (Chiaroscuro).

𝄞 *Listen for*

Dazzling technique; hard-swinging bow-work; tremendous speed and versatility; double (and even quadruple) stops; sparkling sense of humor

💿 *Discography*

Venuti, Joe, *Stringing the Blues* (Koch)

Venuti, Joe, *New York Sessions: 1926–1935* (ESP)

Venuti, Joe, *Classic Columbia and OKeh Recordings of Joe Venuti and Eddie Lang* (Mosaic)

Stephane Grappelli (1908–1997)

French jazz violinist Stephane Grappelli recorded his first album in the early 1930s with legendary guitarist Django Reinhardt and the Hot Club of France. Their work together was classic. In the ensuing decades, Grappelli toured the world many times with his own acoustic ensemble and recorded close to two hundred albums. In fact, Grappelli is the most recorded jazz artist on any instrument. Known for his collaborations on CD with many great musicians, Grappelli recorded with jazz violinists Svend Asmussen, Jean Luc Ponty, Stuff Smith, and Eddie South.

Grappelli is probably the easiest of the jazz violinists for classical violinists to relate to because of his classical sound on the instrument. Thus his work may serve such violinists as a stepping-stone into jazz and improvisation.

𝄞 *Listen for*

Classical-style vibrato; lyrical, melodic soloing; warm tone; exuberant, energy-infused phrasing

🔕 Discography

Grappelli, Stephane, *Django Reinhardt and Stephane Grappelli* (GNP Crescendo)

Grappelli, Stephane (with Stuff Smith and Jean Luc Ponty), *Jazz Violin Summit* (Legacy)

Grappelli, Stephane (with Stuff Smith), *Violins No End* (Original Jazz Classics)

Jean Luc Ponty (b. 1942)

Jean Luc Ponty's career has spanned bebop, jazz, rock, and world music. He was born in Auranches, France, and trained classically, first with his father and then at the Paris Conservatory. Inspired by his love for jazz—including his appreciation for the jazz violin styles of Stephane Grappelli and Stuff Smith—he moved into jazz full-time upon graduation from the Conservatory. Ponty was one of the first owners of the Barcus Berry electric violin, and he gradually moved to the cutting edge of technology in his music by using various electric violin effects.

In the early part of his career, Ponty, more than any other violinist, created a musical bridge from swing violin to a true bebop violin sound. His first album, *Sunday Walk*, became an icon for a whole generation of improvising violinists and a model of how to play modern jazz on violin. Then Ponty moved on to a more commercial venue of amplified, technologically enhanced rock violin, including jazz tinges in a sophisticated, highly arranged band setting. To date, he has recorded close to fifty CDs.

🔊 Listen for

Fusion of jazz and rock styles; use of electronics; funky grooves; original compositions and arrangements; excellent band interaction

💿 Discography

Ponty, Jean Luc, *Cosmic Messenger* (Atlantic)

Ponty, Jean Luc, *Imaginary Voyage* (Atlantic)

Ponty, Jean Luc, *Enigmatic Ocean* (Atlantic)

Additional Jazz String Players

Svend Asmussen, jazz violinist from Denmark, has performed throughout Europe for close to seventy years. He is equally at home with traditional jazz, swing, and modern jazz. Underappreciated in America, he is extremely popular in Europe.

Discography

Asmussen, Svend, *Fiddler Supreme* (Intim)

Asmussen, Svend, *Fit as a Fiddle* (Da Capo)

Asmussen, Svend (with Stephane Grappelli), *Live at Carnegie Hall/June Night* [Live] (Collectables)

Regina Carter, jazz violinist, has distinguished herself as one of the most important popular jazz violinists of today. In addition to her solo work, she has performed with Oliver Lake, Max Roach, the Uptown String Quartet, and the String Trio of New York.

Discography

Carter, Regina, *Motor City Moments* (Polygram)

Carter, Regina (with Kenny Barron), *Freefall* (Universal)

Carter, Regina, *Paganini: After a Dream* (Verve)

Matt Turner, jazz cellist, is regarded as one of the world's leading improvising cellists. Equally adept in many styles, Turner performs everything from jazz standards and twentieth-century new music to alternative rock and improvised avant-garde.

Discography

Turner, Matt, *Infiltrator* (Geode)

Turner, Matt (with Jeff Song & Lowbrow), *Rules of Engagement*
(Asian Improv)

Turner, Matt (with the Scott Fields Ensemble), *Disaster at Sea*
(Music and Arts)

Claude Williams, the oldest living jazz violinist in the world, moved from Muskogee to Kansas City, Oklahoma, when he was twenty to start his career in music. He learned his version of "Cherokee" from Charlie Parker, jammed with Art Tatum, and became known for his 1930s performances on guitar with Count Basie, as well as his violin work with Andy Kirk's Twelve Clouds of Joy and singer Jay McShann. Williams went on to create a solo career that has taken him all over the world.

Discography

Williams, Claude, *Claude Williams Live at J's, Parts 1 and 2* (Arhoolie)

Williams, Claude (with Jay McShann), *The Man from Muskogee*
(Sackville)

Blues and Jazz Strings Today

Blues, swing, modern jazz, and Latin (bossa nova and Afro-Cuban) are all considered essential aspects of the jazz violinists' repertoire. Some players have chosen to emulate the traditional swing violin sound, while others have gone on to create their own original voices on the instrument. Few of today's improvising string players are stylistic purists. Like their predecessors, the blues fiddlers, their musical tastes are quite eclectic. It is not uncommon for string players to combine styles to create their music. For instance, Darol Anger, Mark O'Connor, and Andy Stein dip in and out of fiddle styles, blues, swing, and jazz. Jenny Scheinman draws on a background that includes fiddle, swing, klezmer, and modern jazz. Other players, such as John Blake, Jr., draw on bebop and modern jazz for inspiration. Fusion players, including Jean Luc Ponty and Michal Urbaniak, have experimented with jazz-rock amalgamations. Regina Carter draws on a background that includes Motown, modern jazz, and Latin, and Randy Sabien draws on blues, calypso, fiddle styles, rock, jazz, and his early training as a drummer to create his sound.

photo by Jim McGuire

Mark O'Connor

We are fortunate to be a part of such a creative family. We are only at the crest of the tidal wave. Young players today are growing up surrounded by music spawned by several generations of fertile imaginations. Who knows what is in store for the future!

Additional Support Materials: Jazz Violin

💿 *Play-A-Longs, Volumes 1 through 106* (CDs)

Jamey Aebersold has created over one hundred play-along CDs that offer accompaniments for jazz standards, jazz warm-ups, rhythm changes, blues, and more. (Jamey Aebersold Jazz)

💾 *Band-in-a-Box*

Compatible with PC or Mac, this software program enables the user to create accompaniments in hundreds of styles over any harmonic progression desired. (PG Music)

📖 *Desert Sands: The Recordings and Performances of Stuff Smith* by Anthony Barnett

This book is chock full of biographical material, photographs, interview material, and a full discography. A "must have" for Stuff Smith fans. (AB Fable)

📖 *Improvising Violin* by Julie Lyonn Lieberman*

A comprehensive guide to the art of violin improvisation in jazz, blues, swing, folk, rock, and New Age. This book includes exercises, riffs, techniques, patterns, chord charts, tunes, photos, and quotes. Preface by Darol Anger. (Huiksi Music)

*Also available as an instructional audio series through Homespun Tapes

📖 *Jazz Chord Studies for Violin* by Matt Glaser and Joe Viola

This book presents intermediate to advanced studies and etudes. (Berklee College of Music)

📖 *Jazz Fiddle Wizard: A Practical Guide to Jazz Improvising for Strings* by Martin Norgaard

Presented through a step-by-step jazz violin instruction book and CD, Norgaard's method teaches improvisational patterns and principles while using tunes and chords from standard jazz repertoire. (Mel Bay Publications)

📖 *Jazz Improvisation Made Easy* by John Blake, Jr., and Jody Harmon

This book presents a user-friendly play-along method that teaches jazz improvisation through step-by-step instructions. World-renowned jazz violinist John Blake, Jr., provides examples. Includes companion CD or cassette. (JIME)

📖 *Jazz Philharmonic* by Bob Phillips and Randy Sabien

This series of books is geared toward string orchestra students who are learning their instruments and simultaneously learning basic jazz concepts. Each book presents original tunes with interchangeable parts, backgrounds, bass lines, and solos. Any combination of string instruments will work using this format. Beginning improvisation is handled with preparatory rhythms, scales, and call-and-response. Musical examples are on an accompanying CD, which can be purchased separately. (Alfred Publishing)

📖 *Jazz Violin with Stephane Grappelli* by Matt Glaser

This book includes jazz violin history, a discography, and transcribed solos of six great violinists. Intermediate and advanced. (Oak Publications)

📖 *Past the Print: Discovering Creative Improvisation for String Players* by Julianna Waller

In workbook format, this book features four skill sections: "Playing Melodies by Ear and Transposing," "Sequential Exercises on Chords," "Phrase Development," and "Experiences in Creativity." Waller presents a framework for the creative expansion of musical ideas, skill development required for real-time improvisation, and application of exercises in multiple keys. (Mel Bay Publications)

📖 *Rockin' Out with Blues Fiddle* by Julie Lyonn Lieberman

This book is a comprehensive guide to playing the blues on bowed strings, complete with warm-ups, patterns, pentatonic scales, tunes, and historical information. Includes a practice CD. (Huiksi Music)

📖 *Stuff Smith: Pure at Heart* by Anthony Barnett

This monograph by and about Hezekiah Stuff Smith presents stories and anecdotes from life on the road in Stuff's own words. (AB Fable)

📼 *Swing Fiddle* by Paul Anastasio

In this video, Paul Anastasio teaches how to use forcing, chromatic movement, double neighboring tones, and syncopated patterns. (Ridge Runner)

📼 *Swingin' Jazz Violin* taught by Matt Glaser

Violin players (as well as musicians on any instrument) will benefit from this dynamic, interactive video, developed with the beginning to intermediate player in mind. Includes a music book. (Homespun Tapes)

💿 Supplemental Discography

Ali, Akbar

Black Swan Quartet (Minor Music)

Anger, Darol (also see Turtle Island String Quartet)

The Duo (Rounder)
Tideline (Windham Hill)
Chiaroscuro (Windham Hill)
Fiddlistics (Kaleidoscope)
Psychograss (Windham Hill)

Asmussen, Svend

Hot Fiddle (Brunswick)
Hot Swing Fiddle Classics (Folklyric)
Toots and Svend/Yesterday and Today (A&M)
Svend Asmussen: Amazing Strings (MPS)
Svend Asmussen Spielt Welterfolge (Telefunken)
Duke Ellington's Jazz Violin Session (Atlantic)
Skol (Epic)
Prize Winners (Matrix)

Bacsik, Elek

Bird and Dizzy (Flying Dutchman)
I Love You Bob (Thiele Music)

Bang, Billy

New York Collage (Anima)
Sweet Space (Anima)

Distinction Without a Difference (Hat Hut)
Rainbow Gladiator (Soul Note)
Invitation (Soul Note)
Outline No. 12 (Celluloid)
Bangception (Hat Music)
Fire from Within (Soul Note)
Live at Carlos (Soul Note)
Valve No. 10 (Soul Note)
Tribute to Stuff Smith, Sept. 1992 (Soul Note)

Blake, Jr., John

Maiden Dance (Gramavision)
Rhythm and Blues (Gramavision)
A New Beginning (Rhino)
Adventures of the Heart (Gramavision)

Bluestone, Harry

Artistry in Jazz (Dobre DR)

Brown, Clarence Gatemouth

Clarence Gatemouth Brown (Blackjack)
Clarence Gatemouth Brown: The Original Peacock Recordings, (Rounder)

Compo, Peter

Nostalgia in Times Square (Cadence Jazz)
Live at the West End Cafe (Bean)

Creach, Papa John

Papa John Creach (Grunt)
Rock Father (Buddah)
Playing My Fiddle for You (Grunt)

Delin, Diane

Talking Stick (Blujazz Productions)

Dixon, Akua

Quartette Indigo (Landmark)
Afrika, Afrika with Regina Carter
(Savant)

Eyges, David

Night Leaves (Brownstone)
Captain (Midatlantic)

Goodman, Jerry

Ariel (Private Music)

Glaser, Matt

Jazz Violin Celebration with
Darol Anger and Dave
Balakrishnan (Kaleidoscope)
Play Fiddle Play (Flying Fish)

Grappelli, Stephane

*Django Reinhardt and Stephane
Grappelli: Hot Club of France*
(RCA)
Victor Parisian Swing (GNP)
Django Reinhardt (CLD)
Tea for Two (Angel)
Violins No End with Stuff Smith
(Pablo)

Feelings and Finesse (Atlantic)
I Remember Django (Black Lion)
Limehouse Blues (Black Lion)
Grappelli Meets Barney Kessel
(Black Lion)
Venupelli Blues (Charly)
Homage to Django (Classic Jazz)
Just One of Those Things (Angel)
Parisian Thoroughfare (Black Lion)
Stuff and Slam (Accord)
Reunion with George Shearing
(Polygram)
Stephane Grappelli/Bill Coleman
(Classic Jazz)
Live at Carnegie Hall (Doctor Jazz)
Young Django (Verve)
Live at Tivoli Gardens (Pablo)
Stephane Grappelli and Hank Jones
(Muse)
*Stephane Grappelli and David
Grisman Live* (Warner
Brothers)
Happy Reunion (Rhino)
At the Winery (Concord Jazz)
Live at San Francisco (Black Hawk)
Together at Last (Flying Fish)
Grappelli Plays Jerome Kern (GRP)
One on One with McCoy Tyner
(Milestone)
In Tokyo (Denon)
Stephane Grappelli Meets Earl Hines
(Black Lion)
Paris Encounter (Atlantic)
Shades of Django (Verve)
Fascinating Rhythm (Onyx Classix)

*Menuhin and Grappelli Play
"Jalousie"* (Angel)
Afternoon in Paris (BASF)
Stephane Grappelli 1971
(PYE Popular)
Stephane Grappelli 1973
(PYE Popular)

Hwang, Jason

Caverns (New World)

Invert

Invert (Inverted Music)
Between the Seconds (Capstone
Records)

Jenkins, Leroy

For Players Only (JCOA)
Solo Concert (India Navigation)
Lifelong Ambitions (Black Saint)
Legend of Al Glatson (Black Saint)
Space Mind/New Worlds (Tomato)
Mixed Quintet (Black Saint)

Kennedy, Jr., Joe

Where've You Been? (Concord Jazz)
Magnifique! (Black & Blue)
Trends (Asch Recordings)

LaFlamme, David

Inside Out (Amherst)

Levine, Michael

No Guitars (CMI Music)

Lockwood, Didier

The Didier Lockwood Group
(Gramavision)
Storyboard (Dreyfus)
Tribute to Stephane Grappelli
(Dreyfus)

Luluk

Born Free (Zebra Acoustic)

O'Connor, Mark

Hot Swing Trio, In Full Swing
(Sony Odyssey)
Heroes (Warner Brothers)

Perry, Geoffrey

Fitzhugh and the Fanatics (Fanatical
Fitzhugh Music)
Blue Standards (Fanatical Fitzhugh
Music)

Pointer, Noel

Hold-On (United Artists)
Phantazia (Blue Note)

Ponty, Jean Luc

Violin Summit with Smith,
Grappelli, Asmussen (Verve)
Cantelope Island (Blue Note)
New Violin Summit (MPS)
Upon the Wings of Music (Atlantic)

Jean Luc Ponty and Stephane Grappelli (Verve)

Sunday Walk (BASF)

Enigmatic Ocean (Atlantic)

Electric Connection (World Pacific Jazz)

The Jean-Luc Ponty Experience (World Pacific Jazz)

Aurora (Atlantic)

Upon the Wings of Music (Atlantic)

Cosmic Messenger (Atlantic)

Imaginary Voyage (Atlantic)

Rite of Strings (Capitol)

No Absolute Time (Atlantic)

Ramo, Michéle

Full Moon Above New York City (Ramo Music)

Sabien, Randy

Fiddlehead Blues (Fiddlehead Music)

In a Fog (Fiddlehead Music)

Live at the Cafe Carpe (Fiddlehead Music)

Paintin' the Canvas (Fiddlehead Music)

Segue with Brian Torff (Fiddlehead Music)

The Sound of Fish Dreaming (Fiddlehead Music)

Seifert, Zbigniew

Passion (ST)

Smith, Stuff

Swinging Stuff (Storyville)

Stephane Grappelli and Stuff Smith (Verve)

Live in Paris (FCD)

Live at Montmartre (Storyville)

Stuff Smith (Everest)

The 1943 Trio (Circle)

Black Violin (MPS)

Hot Swing Fiddle Classics (Folklyric)

Have Violin Will Swing (Verve)

Stuff Smith (Verve)

Dizzy Gillespie/Stuff Smith (Verve)

Stuff Smith and Robert Crumb (AB Fable)

Stuff Smith: 1944–1946 Studio, Broadcast, Concert and Apartment Performances (AB Fable)

Soldier String Quartet

Sequence Girls (Rift)

South, Eddie

The Chronological Eddie South 1937–1941 (Classics)

Eddie South: Black Gipsy (Epm Musique)

Djangologie #5 and #6 (EMI)

String Trio of New York

Area Code 212 (Black Saint)

As Tears Go By (ITM)

Ascendant (Vintage Jazz)

Octagon (Black Saint)

Subramaniam, L.

Spanish Wave (Milestone)
Indian Express (Milestone)
Blossom (Crusaders)
Magic Fingers (Ganesh)
Indian Classical Music (Discovery)
Inde Du Sud (Musidisc)
Subramaniam (MAI)

Taylor, Will

RadioEdge (Will Taylor
    Productions)

Turtle Island String Quartet

Spider Dreams (Windham Hill)
Turtle Island String Quartet
    (Windham Hill)
Metropolis (Windham Hill)
Skylife (Windham Hill)
On the Town (Windham Hill Jazz)
Who Do We Think We Are?
    (Windham Hill Jazz)

Uptown String Quartet

Uptown String Quartet (Philips)

Urbaniak, Michal

Fusion (Columbia)
Cinemode (Rykodisc)
Music for Violin and Jazz Quartet
    (JAM)

Venuti, Joe

Joe Venuti with Eddie Lang (JSP)
Joe Venuti and His Violin (Jazz Man)
Violin Jazz (Yazoo)
Stringing the Blues (Sony Special
    Products)
Mad Fiddler from Philly (Shoestring)
Joe Venuti Plays Jerome Kern
    (Golden Crest)
Venupelli Blues (BYG)
Daddy of the Violin (MPS)
Joe & Zoot (Chiaroscuro)
Blue Four (Chiaroscuro)
Hot Sonatas (Chiaroscuro)
Sliding By (Gazell)
Joe in Chicago (Flying Fish)

White, Michael

Father Music Mother Dance
    (Impulse)
Impulse Artists on Tour (Impulse)
Spirit Dance (Impulse)

Williams, Claude

Live at J's Part 1 and 2 (Arhoolie)
Summit '88 (Huiksi Music)
The Man from Muskogee (Sackville)

Zeitlin, Paula

Walk a Little Slower (SAZL Music)

The Cellists' and Violists' Corner

Much of the American history of strings in blues, jazz, and fiddle styles is violin-centric, but you will see that this phenomenon is not paralleled worldwide when you read the chapter "Strings Around the World."

Today's violists and cellists are becoming more and more active in all styles. Overall, cellists have outnumbered violists in their exploration of blues and jazz. From the free-flowing improvisations of David Darling and Eugene Friesen to the stylistically broad experimentation of improvising cellist Matt Turner, cellists are constantly exploring their instruments in new ways. Cellists such as Martha Colby pluck walking bass lines, and Mark Summer of Turtle Island String Quartet has adapted the bluegrass fiddler's chop technique to create a highly percussive use of the instrument. David Eyges improvises with a textural and atonal voice on the instrument, and Akua Dixon plays straight-ahead and modern jazz on cello with the Quartette Indigo. Erik Friedlander, equally at home in modern jazz and classical, has been called one of today's most ingenious and forward-thinking cellists.

Violists of note include Danny Seidenberg and Katrina Wreede, both originally members of Turtle Island String Quartet and

> The viola sustains a prominent position in Scandinavian and Eastern European music.

both of whom have moved on to create solo careers. Tanya Kalmanovitch, a Juilliard graduate, is another exceptional violist who is at home in a wide range of musical styles, and electric violist Martha Mooke has pioneered original music for electric strings.

We can clearly expect more contributions and involvement from the viola and cello communities in the future.

Support Materials: Cello

📖 *BackUp Trax: Old Time and Fiddle Tunes for Cello*
by Dix Bruce

Arranged and performed by cellist Renata Bratt, this book and companion CD include fourteen melodies. The tunes are presented on the recording first at a slow speed with guitar only, then at a normal speed with an entire band. Split-track mixing allows students to hear just the melody, just the rhythm section, or both. Finally, the band plays several choruses, allowing students to play the leads. (Mel Bay Publications)

📖 *The Cello Fiddling Tune Book* by Deborah Greenblatt

This book presents transcriptions of twenty-seven tunes, including hoedowns, waltzes, polka, rags, and jigs. Includes chord symbols. (Greenblatt and Seay)

📖 *Fat Notes* by Rodney Farrar

Presenting works ranging from Bach to the blues, this is a fun collection of pieces, arranged for groups containing cellists of different levels. Includes a companion CD with quality recordings of the arrangements. (New Directions Cello Association)

📖 *The Fiddling Cellist* by Renata Bratt

This method book for cello presents "fiddle" tunes in a number of different styles, including Irish, old-time, and bluegrass. Each tune, arranged for two or three cellos, is accompanied by a short study teaching idiomatic bass lines and back-up harmony, as well as improvisational soloing over the chord changes. The companion CD includes guitar accompaniments for all tunes. (Mel Bay Publications)

📖 *Jazz Cello* by Chris White

White's method, presented in this book and companion CD, is designed to help cellists develop as well-rounded players. White teaches melodies, bass lines, and chords, as well as improvisation in swing, blues, and Latin jazz styles. The companion CD includes accompaniments with piano, bass, and drums. (Cello Works)

📖 *Jazz Cello Wizard* by Martin Norgaard

A step-by-step jazz improvisation method for all beginning improvisers, this book and companion CD present basic skills in a fun and easy-to-hear and -play manner. The book includes three elementary jazz tunes arranged for groups of any size or instrumentation and is well suited for use in a classroom or by studio teachers. (Mel Bay Publications)

📖 *Jazz Expressions and Explorations* by David Baker

David Baker is one of the most sought-after jazz educators in the world, and this is his most innovative book yet on the art of jazz improvisation. The text emphasizes the patterns and phrases that work best for cellists and, systematically studied, will allow for greater musical expression. (Jamey Aebersold Jazz)

📖 *What! For Cello?* by Sean Grissom

Consisting of transcriptions of five tunes with three-part cello arrangements and solo lines, this book presents contemporary music for teachers and their students. Includes a practice tape. (Endpin Music Publishing)

💿 Discography: Cello

Abramsky, David, *A World of Good* (DSA)

Darling, David, *Cello Blue* (Hearts of Space)

Darling, David, *Eight-String Religion* (Wind Over the Earth)

Dixon, Akua, *Quartette Indigo* (Landmark)

Dixon, Akua, with Regina Carter, *Afrika, Afrika* (Savant)

Een, Robert, *Your Life Is Not Your Own* (Buzzbox)

Een, Robert, *Fertile Fields* (Buzzbox)

Een, Robert, *The Rook* (Buzzbox)

Eyges, David, *Night Leaves* (Brownstone)

Eyges, David, *Captain* (Midatlantic)

Fennell, Muneer B., *Confidentially Speaking* (Seraphon)

Freudmann, Gideon, *Ukrainian Pajama Party* (Gadfly)

Freudmann, Gideon, *A-Dobe Dog House* (Gadfly)

Freudmann, Gideon, *Cellobotomy* (Gadfly)

Friedlander, Erik, *Topaz* (Siam)

Friedlander, Erik, *Skin* (Siam)

Friesen, Eugene, *In the Shade of Angels* (FiddleTalk Music)

Friesen, Eugene, *The Song of Rivers* (FiddleTalk Music)

Grissom, Sean, *Jambalaya Jive* (Endpin Music)

Grissom, Sean, *From the Street* (EMP)

Grissom, Sean, *Just Cello* (EMP)

Haas, Natalie, with Alasdair Fraser, *Legacy of the Scottish Fiddle, Vol. 1* (Culburnie)

Haas, Natalie, with Alasdair Fraser, *Legacy of the Scottish Fiddle, Vol. 2* (Culburnie)

Hawkes, Pete, *Melancholy Cello* (IAG)

Longsworth, Eric, *I Hear You* (Pascale Graham Productions)

Marshall, Kye, *Winter's End* (Zephyr/Westwind Productions)

McFarland-Johnson, Jeffrey, *Cellektra Fertilization* (JohnSong Music)

Nakipbekova, Alfia, with James Hesford, *Cellorythmics: Invasion* (Meta)

Newton, Abby, *Castles, Kirks, and Caves, Scottish Music of the 18th Century* (Redwing Music)

Rasputina, *Thanks for the Ether* (Sony)

Rasputina, *Transylvania Regurgitations* (Sony)

Roberts, Hank, *I'll Always Remember* (Level Green)

Schefczyk, *Cellofire* (Schachblume)

Sieber, Jami, *Lush Mequanique* (Out Front Music)

Trajko, Artur, with Jacco Muller, *Silueta* (Mihrab)

Turner, Matt, *Never, Never Now* (Stellar Sound Productions)

Turner, Matt, *Crushed Smoke* (Tautology)

Turner, Matt, *Outside In* (Stellar Sound Productions)

Turner, Matt, *The Mouse That Roared* (Stellar Sound Productions)

Von Cello, *Breaking the Sound Barriers* (Von Cello)

White, Chris, *Cello Again* (Cello Works)

White, Chris, and the Cayuga Jazz Ensemble, *First Principles*
(Cello Works)

Woodwork, *Viewfinder* (Edible)

Support Materials: Viola

📖 *Fiddle Tunes for Beginning Viola* by Stacy Phillips

This book presents thirty fiddle tunes arranged for viola. (Mel Bay
Publications)

📖 *Fiddle Tunes for Two Violas* by Stacy Phillips

Fifty-six tunes, featuring old-time, waltzes, bluegrass, jigs, rags,
swing tunes, and polkas, are included in this book. Supported by
accompaniments on CD. (Mel Bay Publications)

📖 *Jazz Viola Wizard* by Martin Norgaard

A step-by-step jazz improvisation method for all beginning improvisers, this book and companion CD presents basic skills in a fun and
easy-to-hear and -play manner. The book includes three elementary
jazz tunes arranged for groups of any size or instrumentation and
is well suited for use in a classroom or by studio teachers. (Mel
Bay Publications)

📖 *The Viola Fiddling Book* by Deborah Greenblatt

This book contains transcriptions of twenty-seven tunes, including
hoedowns, waltzes, polka, rags, and jigs. Includes chord symbols.
(Greenblatt and Seay)

📖 *Violaerobics: A Technical Workout for Violists* by Katie
Wreede

Violaerobics uses a warm-up/workout/cool-down approach with
patterns in all keys over scales, arpeggios, orchestral excerpts, and
jazz licks. The book presents ear-training and left- and right-hand
techniques, as well as stretching and relaxation. Transcribed for
violin, too. (MMB Music)

🔵 Discography: Viola

Kalmanovitch, Tanya, *Hut Five* (Perspicacity)

Mooke, Martha, *Cafe Mars* (Vener Music)

Mooke, Martha, *Enharmonic Vision* (Vener Music)

Mooke, Martha, *Klezmer Concerto and Encores* (Naxos)

Seidenberg, Danny, with Turtle Island String Quartet, *Art of the Groove* (Koch International Classics)

Seidenberg, Danny, with Turtle Island String Quartet, *String Quartet: A Windham Hill Retrospective* (Windham Hill)

Strings in Popular Music   *6*

The day rock legend Buddy Holly used a string section on "Raining in My Heart" (1958), he inaugurated a new adventure for bowed strings. Although jazz saxophonist Charlie Parker had already incorporated a string section into his work ten years earlier, strings had not yet been used to complement rock and pop. Now everyone jumped on the bandwagon, from the big-name crooners to the Beatles.

Even with this apparent breakthrough, however, the legato/ vibrato stereotype associated with classical bowed strings continued to prevail. In addition, players were still expected to perform and record as anonymous chart-reading machines. Producers and arrangers could not conceptualize the use of strings beyond their historic Western European role.

It was blues/jazz violinists such as Papa John Creach and Sugarcane Harris in the 1950s, as well as sixties fusion artists including Seatrain's Richard Greene, the Flock's Jerry Goodman, and Jean Luc Ponty, who helped distinguish the violin as an independent voice equal to electric guitar. These players also set the precedent for the violinist as bandleader in the popular genre, in league with a jazz violin tradition that had already been established in the late twenties and early thirties by players such as Joe Venuti, Eddie South, and Stuff Smith.

As the violin became a vehicle for name artists to feature themselves as soloists, bands started integrating string players into their stage shows rather than constantly leaving them in the shadows. String players began contributing rhythmic backup and textures through electronic effects. Rather than wearing inconspicuous clothing, they adapted their dress to match popular fashion.

Thus violin assumed the lead in the "popular string revolution." Close to three decades later, cello caught up. From the 1980s through recent years, artists such as Von Cello and the group Rasputina, along with fusion cellists such as Matt Turner and David Darling, have helped distinguish the cello as an equal in versatility to the violin. Interestingly, the invention of five-to seven-string violins relegated the viola as such to a background seat.

In any case, the rock string sound has evolved from pretty, lyrical, and harmonic to gutsy, funky, dynamic, percussive, and awesome!

Why Add Popular Music to Your Curriculum?

Practically speaking, your string students stand a greater chance today of earning a good living playing strings for recording sessions, rock tours, radio and television jingles, and social functions than as classical soloists or in orchestras or chamber music groups. You also stand a far greater chance when you integrate popular music into your curriculum of maintaining student interest, preventing attrition, and servicing community events through student performances.

Rock Versus Pop: What Is the Difference?

The term *pop* refers to whatever musical style is currently popular. Big Band swing music was the pop music of the 1930s and 1940s. Elements of blues, R&B (rhythm and blues), and country music merged to produce rock, which has maintained its pop status for over fifty years. Radio stations banned rock artists until disc jockeys accepted payoffs, referred to by the major record labels as "payola," to play their music.

It is strange how a music that is so popular defies uniform categorization. For every band that is electric, there is an acoustic counterpart; singers range from shouting and screaming to crooning, rapping, or lyrical singing; lyrics can vary from confessional to narrative to poetry. Band size ranges from singers accompanying themselves to large ensembles with brass, mini-chorus, full rhythm sections, and more. Rock 'n' roll was only homogeneous for a few years before it began spinning off new styles and variations. In fact, there are well over one hundred "rock" styles.

Radio and television play an incredibly vital role in defining what a young person should listen to today. As educators, we can pay attention to and take advantage of students' taste in music by helping them analyze and differentiate between radio-friendly styles that have been packaged for commercial consumption and artists or bands that emphasize true musicianship and craft. We can achieve this by exposing them to options through both listening and playing sessions.

Common Traits

Given the extreme differences between both ensembles and stylistic characteristics, we can focus in the classroom on certain shared traits. For instance, most of the music in the pop/rock genre is in 4/4; few pieces

Partial List of Rock Styles

Adult Alternative Pop/Rock	Goth Rock
Alternative Country-Rock	Grunge
	Hard Rock
Alternative Metal	Hardcore Punk
Blues-Rock	Heartland Rock
Boogie Rock	Heavy Metal
British Invasion	Hip Hop
British Metal	Indie Pop
British Psyche-delia	Indie Rock
	Jazz-Rock
British Punk	Latin Rock
British Trad Rock	Motown
Britpop	R&B
Contemporary R&B	Psychedelic Pop
	Punk Metal
Country-Rock	Rap
Disco	Rockabilly
Doo Wop	Singer/Song-writer
Early British Pop/Rock	Ska Revival
	Soft Rock
Experimental Rock	Southern Rock
	Sunshine Pop
Folk-Pop	Surf
Folk-Rock	Swedish Pop/Rock
Funk Metal	
Garage Punk	Symphonic Black Metal
Garage Rock	
Girl Group	Teen Idol
Glitter Go-Go	Tex-Mex
Goth Metal	Urban Folk

115

are exclusively instrumental, because the topical content conveyed by the singer is essential to the art form; the harmonic progressions are generally simple; and the instruments' jobs are to either create a rhythmic/harmonic backdrop, to frame the vocals, or to solo.

Sheet Music for Amplified Strings

The need for amplification in the rock band context developed for practical reasons: an acoustic instrument pitted against solid-body guitar, drums, sax, and the like cannot project. It gets lost in the mix. A wooden instrument with a mounted pickup or a clip-on mike is sufficient for a small acoustic ensemble, but, in order to get enough volume boost to play with a larger group or electric instruments, a solid-body instrument is necessary. It doesn't matter what the amplified violin or cello is built out of (it is the electronics and an accurate fingerboard that are essential), enabling makers to be creative with designs. The rising need for solid-body violins and cellos has cultivated a thriving market.

When first transitioning into rock, many players get confused as to the role an amplified instrument plays in the genre. They think that there is special music written for electric violin or cello. This misconception leads them to believe that if they can locate the correct music, they will suddenly sound like a rock player. How you play and what you play on are two distinctly different affairs. You could play on an electric violin using classical technique and simply sound like an amplified classical violinist. Conversely, there are techniques that can make you "rock out" on an acoustic instrument (genre-specific riffs, ponticello coupled with a pentatonic pattern, and so on).

While there are a few composers and companies offering music created specifically for rock strings, such as Mark Wood and Mona Lisa Music, it won't sound much like rock unless players learn the techniques that embody the musical style and learn how to improvise. You can provide quick, easy assistance to younger students who aren't ready to tackle genre-specific playing skills by using digital delay, phase shifter, distortion, and other rock-oriented electronic effects, giving them the illusion that they sound like rock 'n' rollers and thereby inspiring them to spend more time on-instrument.

Preparation for the Rock Band

We tend to rely so heavily on sheet music in our string classes and orchestra rehearsals and concerts that we can easily miss the potential to offer something new when teaching popular idioms. While sheet music can grant the illusion of playing in a rock style, in truth, it only provides notation for the melody with a fun arrangement that derives its key components from the rock band sound. In the real world, the string player rarely plays the melody of the song, because that is the vocalist's job. To prepare our students for the "real thing," we have to train them to sit in with a band. This involves teaching them how to listen to the bass line, how to capture the groove created by the drummer or percussionist, how to locate the tonal center of each song, and so on.

Many rock bands aren't articulate about keys, chords, structure, or even expectations regarding the string player's role. String players can cultivate six skills to prepare themselves for playing in a rock band:

1. The ability to quickly find the tonal center of the piece

Unlike many jazz tunes, most rock tunes maintain a single tonal center. You can train your students by putting on random selections from CDs by their favorite bands and encouraging them to search for a held pitch that will work against most of the first verse. Once they have found the tonal center, they can try a major, minor, mixolydian, or pentatonic scale against the verse to sketch out the notes that will most likely work well for their solo. This provides the class with a wonderful opportunity to learn about different types of scales in a hands-on rather than an academic learning style.

2. The ability to sketch out the overall structure

Give your students a piece of blank or music paper, and, as a group, count out the number of measures per verse and the number of verses, and note whether or not there is a change in tonal center. (If there is one, ask students to mark where it occurs.) Encourage them to invent their own method of notation. Here is an example of notes I made during a 1984 recording session with pop star Laura Nyro:

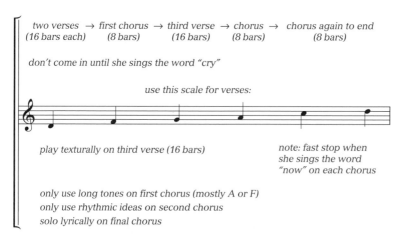

3. The ability to locate the heartbeat or groove of the piece and support it while playing backup or highlight it while soloing

Using pencils or chopsticks held like drumsticks, encourage students to tap out the rhythms they hear while listening to a popular song. Then ask them to try to imitate those rhythms on a single pitch with their bows.

Now ask them to focus their listening on the bass line. Let them experiment on their instruments, trying to duplicate a segment of the bass line. In this context, it is extremely helpful to use PG Music's Band-in-a-Box because you can mute the other instruments, highlight the bass line, and even slow the accompaniment down (see page 124 for sample bass lines).

4. The ability to create a riff or series of riffs that blend well

From reading notated music for years, we have inadvertently been trained to hear in a linear melodic orientation. In addition to drawing upon those skills, string players will need to be able to invent repetitious phrases that create a groove. Such a riff or phrase only needs a handful of notes to be successful. It is the tangential rhythm and the repetition that give it drive.

5. The ability to support vocal music

The string player can play backup behind the singer (taking care not to obscure the lyrics), play fillers (tasty phrases that either echo the melody or react to it) to dress up the space between the verses, or improvise a solo. It is essential to know about and prepare for all three and to ask the lead singer or bandleader to indicate his or her preference.

6. The ability to improvise a solo

Soloing is contagious. At first, no one wants to feel like a fool in front of the class, so most students will desperately shake their heads "no" when called upon to solo. If you simplify, turning the process into a game, students won't want to stop once they get the hang of it.

Try putting on an accompaniment (see "Support Materials: Music-Minus-One" in chapter 8) or a popular music CD—preferably one that a student has recommended.

Ask each student to play two notes for four beats in as many ways as possible, then three notes, then four, and so on. Each time you rotate through the class, students will have learned more from one another, they will be more familiar with hearing in four-bar groupings (a popular framework for soloing in all styles), and they will feel more confident when asked to play in longer phrases, such as eights or sixteens. If you are working with a particularly shy class, use call and response by playing a two-note idea, asking students to repeat it back, and then adding notes in successively each time the class has successfully captured the previous line.

Stylistic Characteristics

A good rock string player has to develop a number of skills involving articulation of the bow and left-hand that are different from those required by classical. These include:

1. Rock vibrato

The width and speed of the vibrato should be tempered to achieve the desired effect. Rather than creating a consistently smooth vibrato throughout, the soloist can also use what is often referred to in rock strings as a "wide, hysterical motion" on the surface of the string, or a slow, wide roll. It is best to learn to play without vibrato altogether so that it can be used as a sound effect rather than as the principal note-to-note accessory.

2. Slide technique

Students should be encouraged to master a range of slides into and out of notes. Using width and speed as the variables, have them experiment with varying the entrance into notes they wish to emphasize by sliding the finger lightly on the string up into or down out of the desired pitch. It is also useful for players to practice leaning down out of a pitch and back up into it or sliding between two pitches to transit between two notes.

3. Pentatonic and diminished pathways

Pentatonic runs are very popular in the rock idiom, as are the diminished arpeggios and scales. These scales and patterns can be superimposed over unrelated chords and sound good as long as the improvised line is ultimately resolved back into the key in which the band is playing. This may sound mysterious or complicated, but it isn't. The reason it works is that the pattern being played is consistent unto itself, so it makes sense, musically speaking. When the phrase ends on a note within the key, the pattern is vindicated in retrospect.

While scales can be extremely helpful to establish the "lay of the land," patterns are an important stepping-stone towards breaking out of diatonic (step-wise) movement into more fluid, melodic shapes. Therefore, familiarizing themselves with these pathways on the fingerboard, through practicing scales and patterns in primary keys such as G, D, A, and E, will help prepare players for improvisation in popular styles.

Examples:

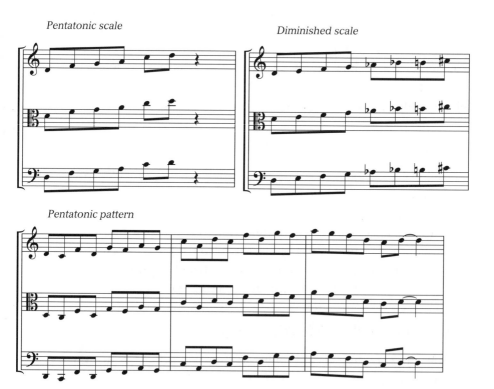

Pentatonic scale

Diminished scale

Pentatonic pattern

Diminished pattern

4. Horizontal fingerings

When we learn how to shift, we tend to play melodic lines vertically. We shift in a straight line up the E string to play the higher pitches and come back down the same way. To develop riff-oriented ideas, it is helpful to practice musical phrases by placing the first finger on the tonic and moving back and forth across two strings.

5. Rhythmic backup

Rather than standing awkwardly between solos, the string player can learn how to develop a strong rhythmic ability, playing backup for other instrumental solos or behind the vocalist. Encourage students to practice scales, patterns, riffs, and repetitious rhythmic ideas against a rock 'n' roll backbeat supplied by a rhythm machine such as the Yamaha QY drum machine or a computer midi file such as those generated by the program Band-in-a-Box by PG Music.

6. Playing on an amplified or electric instrument

Approach your school about purchasing electric instruments, including at least one four-string violin, one five- to seven-string violin, and one cello. This way, students will have a chance to familiarize themselves with how to plug in instruments, how to use an amp, and the lighter touch an amplified instrument can require.

7. Bass lines

It is extremely useful for students to learn to play bass lines. This skill can be taught by copying lines off of recordings. In addition to developing a keener understanding of the bass player's role in the band (and therefore being able to pay attention to his or her lines more distinctly while soloing), this learning process strengthens the soloist's ability to provide support to other soloists by playing background lines.

1.

8. Electronic effects

You can purchase separate effects such as chorus, flange, digital delay, and distortion. Use the Internet or your local music store to research the possibilities, and give your students a chance to work with some or all of these effects. Each effect creates a new sound environment that students can experiment with. An effects box called the Zoom box contains dozens of effects built into one unit and is an economical place to start.

Amplification

Back in the 1920s, jazz violinist Stuff Smith had to leave Jelly Roll Morton's band after just a couple of days because no one could hear him. We have come a long way. The proliferation of options for amplification has made it challenging to know what to use.

During my "How to Amplify Bowed Strings for Jazz Band" clinic, presented at the International Association of Jazz Educator's 2002 Conference in Long Beach, California, it was interesting to hear the opinions and demonstrations of a line-up of twelve established string players. Each artist demonstrated a different pickup system or solid-body instrument as he or she wailed on the blues. At the clinic we heard Randy Sabien using the L.R. Baggs system on violin followed by Tanya Kalmanovitch on L.R. Baggs for viola; then Aaron Weinstein on the Kurmann soundpost system; Darol Anger on the Eric Aceto violin; Scott Schoeffel on the Mark Wood Viper violin; Martin Norgaard on a five-string Tucker violin; Cathy Morris on a seven-string purple Jordan violin and Yehudit on a five-string Jordan violin; Christian Howes on the Yamaha Silent Violin and Dr. Lou Fischer on the Yamaha silent bass; and, finally, Reva Kuzmich premiered the Sam Ash Quiet Violin. I represented the acoustic violin through a microphone to illustrate the contrast between acoustic and electric.

Many of us shared that we had tried a number of different systems before finally finding our ideal setup. In addition to hearing each instrument side by side (a cassette tape of the clinic is available through the IAJE), one of the highlights of the clinic was hearing players speak about what they initially looked for and why they chose their present systems. This proved how different each of our needs are. It was also exciting to hear the same instrument through each of the ten different amps that Sam Ash kindly provided. This established how the same instrument can offer diverse tonalities, depending upon what kind of system it goes through.

Here are some of the criteria you can use when considering a system for you or your student program.

Why Amplify?

When we become involved with contemporary styles, this often means playing in ensembles that are not typical to the history of bowed strings. The moment we begin to play with horns, drums, or larger mixed ensembles, it becomes harder and harder to hear or be heard. This leads to pressing down too hard on the instrument, which is very taxing on the muscles, or to playing out of tune because we can't hear ourselves well enough to adjust pitch. Amplification solves these problems.

For student players, using amplified instruments introduces an element of playfulness and fun and links players to the musical styles they tend to listen to most, as well as to the technological world we now live in. In addition, the look of the instruments can make students stand out and feel special.

Budget

Before choosing a system, establish what you or your program can afford to pay. Make sure you factor in the cost of an amp (or amps), a preamp if you desire more detailed tonal control, and some cables to use to plug into the amp.

Volume

Assess the environment the students will be rehearsing or performing in, such as band size, instrumentation, and whether they will play solo or with a group of string players. There are limits to how much volume one can achieve from a pickup mounted on the instrument without encountering feedback or distortion. There is a trade-off involved in choosing a solid-body, which can project a lot of volume but tends to eliminate the acoustic tonal quality. It will, quite literally, sound electric. These are important considerations before committing a precious part of your budget.

Timbre

Each system will either change or enhance the acoustic sound. Solid-body instruments offer a completely different tone, as in the difference between an acoustic and electric guitar. A microphone or clip-on mike will give the truest representation of an instrument, with the Kurmann soundpost system coming in a close second, then the L.R. Baggs System if accompanied by its sophisticated Para Acoustic DI preamp. Transducer bridges, such as the Barbera bridge, offer a warmer sound in general than solid-body, but so much of this is influenced by the preamp and amp that it is important when possible to try it all out at a local music store or a colleague's school before investing in a full system.

Standard approaches to amplification

+ Play into a standing microphone or use a small clip-on mike (wireless is an option)

+ Attach a pickup to the bridge or soundpost

+ Buy a transducer bridge and mount it on the instrument

+ Purchase a solid-body electric, which has no acoustic sound and must be plugged into an amp

Available Systems

Let's look more closely at the different systems:

Pickups

Pickups that attach to the instrument's bridge are excellent for a modest boost. Without a preamp,

128

they will provide enough power to be heard in a small club or with a small ensemble, but, in most cases, they give little ability to boost beyond that without distortion. Some pickups can potentially ruin the bridge or push it out of place because of how they attach, so factor that in when choosing a system. You will have to watch your students' instruments carefully.

Transducer bridges

A transducer bridge is a violin, viola, or cello bridge that has the electronics built into it. It usually has a wire coming out of the bridge that subsequently attaches to a fixture that looks like a chin rest mechanism. One end of a cord is plugged into that fixture and the other into a preamp or amp. The transducer bridge generally boosts the outgoing signal more than a pickup.

Sometimes the use of a transducer bridge can alter one's tone (for better or worse) when playing, but it can be mounted on a second, cheaper instrument so as not to interfere with your primary acoustic instrument. The cost of having the bridge shaped by a luthier to fit the instrument must be factored in when using a L.R. Baggs bridge.

Solid-body instruments

The solid-body has little or no sound when played acoustically. It has to be plugged into an amp to be heard. There is no danger of feedback when boosting the volume, and most solid-body instruments will provide all necessary volume. One can also choose between fairly tame-looking instruments and really flashy designs that distinguish a player when he or she steps onto the stage. Before purchasing a solid-body instrument, it is important to make sure that it isn't too heavy or uncomfortable to play.

Solid-body with MIDI

A MIDI-capable instrument is one that has the built-in technology to emit signals that can communicate with compatible electronics. For instance, Zeta sells a MIDI violin that can enable your students to activate the sounds of any instrument in the orchestra by triggering those sounds through the Zeta synthesizer. This setup will give students access to multitudes of sounds, including drums, horns, woodwinds, pianos, guitars, basses, and special effects. The volume of the synthesizer and instrument is controlled entirely from the Zeta instrument; a mixing board or volume pedal is not needed.

MIDI technology can also communicate with music software computer programs, such as Finale by Coda Music, that can transcribe what your students play to help them develop their own compositions.

The Preamp

The preamp is a small box that can be used as an intermediary between the pickup and either an amp or a house system. It provides the capability to boost the volume and also supplies the player with close-at-hand control over the equalization (treble and bass ratios). Note that each pickup system comes with its own companion pre-amp. Mixing equipment from different companies won't provide satisfactory results.

Major Considerations

+ Budget
+ Volume
+ Timbre
+ Comfort

The Amp

No pickup or solid-body is effective without an amp. Purchasing decisions should be based on budget, volume requirements, tone, and transportation concerns (amps can be heavy). Extra guitar cords should always be kept on hand. Because string players need to hear themselves in order to play in tune, players should either place their amps directly behind themselves on a chair or put them in front and tilt them back to face up towards themselves. Otherwise it will be difficult to play in tune over a large ensemble.

Electronic Effects

Electronic effects come in boxes that instruments can be plugged into to change their overall sound. Digital delay, which creates an echo; phase shifter, which fattens the sound and gives it a spatial quality; and octaver, which adds a second interval (usually an octave, although it can be tuned to any other interval) are just a few of the effects available in either a small box or rack-mountable size. The Zoom box is relatively inexpensive and offers a wide range of effects to choose from.

> **Amplification Companies**
>
> See www.amadeuspress.com for links to over a dozen electric violin and cello makers and vendors.

The Use of Fine Tuners

Beyond the fact that well-fitted pegs are generally not a luxury found on instruments in a $2,500 and under range, fine tuners are a must when it comes to playing on an amplified instrument. The use of fine tuners for each of the four strings is an excellent way to make fast, subtle adjustments. The Thomastik tailpiece or a Wittner Ultra with four built-in fine tuners are both good options.

Artist Sampler

Papa John Creach (1917–1994)

One of ten children, John Creach was born in Beaver Falls, Pennsylvania. In 1935, the Creach family moved to Chicago, Illinois, where Creach began playing in bars and clubs. He relocated to Los Angeles, California, in 1945, where he married and played diverse jobs in clubs and films, on a luxury cruiser, and so forth. At age fifty, he struck up a friendship with Joey Covington, who gave him the nickname "Papa John." When Covington joined Jefferson Airplane, he introduced Papa John to the band.

Papa John Creach was a fifty-three-year-old jazz and blues fiddler who had been playing professionally for more than thirty years when he was "discovered" by Jefferson Airplane in 1970. He was so admired by his colleagues that he became a fixture of the Airplane, Hot Tuna, Jefferson Starship, and, as a septuagenarian, Jefferson Starship—The Next Generation. The only violinist to garner a hit single on radio, "Over the Rainbow," he appeared on Hot Tuna's *First Pull Up, Then Pull Down* (1971) and *Burgers* (1973), before he launched his solo career in 1971.

Papa John remained on friendly terms with Starship, recording with them on *Dragon Fly* (1974) and *Red Octopus* (1975). The latter featured another instrumental showcase, "Git Fiddler," which he wrote. He also guested with Jefferson Starship during its spring 1978 tour. Ten years later, he was present at the legendary "Hot Tuna and Friends" concert, at which Paul Kanter and Grace Slick reunited with Jorma Kaukonen and Jack Casady. Papa John suffered a heart attack during the Los Angeles earthquake in January 1994 and passed away on February 22. He was seventy-six years old.

Shortly before Papa John died, he told me that in the early years audiences in most venues would roll their eyes when he arrived with his violin case. They thought a violin was only capable of sweet classical sounds. He liked nothing more than to calmly plug his violin into an amp, turn the volume all the way up, and blast the audience on the first song, just to see the look of shock and delighted surprise on their faces!

◉ Listen for

Funky textures; gutsy, bluesy tone; slide technique; rock-guitaresque lines; a man who loved to play

---

◉ Solo Discography

Creach, Papa John, *Papa John Creach* (One Way)

Creach, Papa John, *I'm the Fiddle Man* (One Way)

Creach, Papa John, *Papa Blues* (Bee Bump)

Creach, Papa John, *Rock Father* (One Way)

Creach, Papa John, *The Best of Papa John Creach* (Kama Sutra/Buddah)

Don "Sugarcane" Harris (1938–1999)

Born in Pasadena, California, Sugarcane started out in the doo-wop group the Squires, which included his childhood friend Dewey Terry. The two broke off and Sugarcane became the guitar-playing half of the 1950s rock duo Don and Dewey. Although the group's songs became hits for other artists, including the Righteous Brothers, Sugarcane switched from guitar to violin when the duo wasn't able to achieve its own success. Classically trained as a violinist, his skill at improvisation began attracting attention from the rock world. He appeared on records by John Lee Hooker, Frank Zappa, Little Richard, the Olympics, the Premiers, Dale and Grace, and Johnny Otis. In 1970, Sugarcane joined forces with British blues musician John Mayall. He also recorded a series of solo albums for labels such as Epic and Polydor. Harris was given the nickname "Sugarcane" by bandleader Johnny Otis.

𝄞 Listen for

An aggressive, electric style—the same sort of vitality that an electric guitar would have; pentatonic riffs that will make your soul dance (he squeezed more out of a few notes than most artists achieve with thousands)

💿 Discography

Harris, Don "Sugarcane," *Sugarcane* (Acadia)

Harris, Don "Sugarcane," with John Mayall, *Back to the Roots* (Polydor)

Harris, Don "Sugarcane," with John Mayall, *Rock the Blues Tonight* (Castle Music America)

Harris, Don "Sugarcane," with Johnny Otis, *Johnny Otis Blues and Swing Party Vol. 1* (J&T)

Harris, Don "Sugarcane," with Johnny Otis, *Cold Shot* (J&T)

Harris, Don "Sugarcane," with Frank Zappa, *Weasels Ripped My Flesh* (Rykodisc)

Harris, Don "Sugarcane," with Frank Zappa, *Hot Rats* (Rykodisc)

Harris, Don "Sugarcane," with Sonny Terry and Brownie McGhee, *Sonny & Brownie* (A&M)

Mark Wood (b. 1956)

In an industry where originality is a precious commodity, recording artist, performer, producer, inventor, and Emmy-winning composer Mark Wood is truly an original. Leaving behind a full classical scholarship at the Juilliard School of Music, Wood set out to realize his personal vision of a "new music." This vision was built on his insatiable need to carve out a niche for the electric violin in rock 'n' roll.

Wood began designing and building violins that better fit this new direction. His inventiveness is epitomized by his wholly unique six- and nine-string fretted double-neck electric violin, "the Violator." Although he has custom-designed and built numerous violins, it was the use of the double-necked electric on his CD *Voodoo Violince* that enabled Wood to shatter all previously held notions of violin sound by pushing far into the realm of sustain, volume, and tonality normally reserved for the electric guitar. The result of these efforts is Wood Violins, a company whose mission is to make Wood's incredible instruments available to the general public. Wood Violins has become highly successful in custom manufacturing and selling the revolutionary, patented Viper electric violin.

♫ *Listen for*

Dexterity; ferocity; texture and attack; electricity; passion; innovation

💿 Discography
Wood, Mark, *Against the Grain* (Guitar Recordings)
Wood, Mark, *Voodoo Violince* (Guitar Recordings)

Additional Popular Violinists

Mindy Jostyn, violinist, has performed with Carly Simon, Billy Joel, and John Mellencamp.

Discography

Jostyn, Mindy, *Cedar Lane* (Moonboy)
Jostyn, Mindy, *Blue Stories* (Moonboy)

Lorenza Ponce, violinist, has performed with Sheryl Crow, Bon Jovi, Kitaro, and John Tesh.

Discography

Ponce, Lorenza, *The Instrumentals* (Melodia)
Ponce, Lorenza, *Mystic Fiddler* (Melodia)
Ponce, Lorenza, *Song of Songs* (Spring Hill Music)

Scarlet Rivera, violinist, has performed with Bob Dylan, the Indigo Girls, Keb Mo, and Tracy Chapman.

Discography

Rivera, Scarlet, *Celtic Spirit* (Western Eagle Foundation)
Rivera, Scarlet, *Behind the Crimson Veil* (Western Eagle Foundation)

Additional Support Materials: Popular Strings

📖 *Beyond Classical Violin* by Charlie Bisharat
An introduction to the world of improvisation, this book/CD pack offers every violinist the tools necessary to play improvised music. The materials contain valuable information about groove and feel,

playing over chord changes, and extended techniques. Musical examples are in the styles of Shankar, Grappelli, Goodman, and Ponty. Styles covered include jazz, blues, rock, popular, ethnic, and world music. (Cherry Lane Music)

📖 *Fiddle Jam: A Way-Cool Easy Way to Learn How to Improvise* by Geoffrey Fitzhugh Perry

This book/CD pack is designed so that a first year student can participate as well as classically trained professional players. Styles include jazz, blues, rock, Cajun, funk, and other hybrid styles. Perry also presents two-string symmetrical fingering blocks called "EZ-Zones" to help encourage the new improviser into a non-thinking, creative state. (Hal Leonard)

📖 *Improvising Violin* with Julie Lyonn Lieberman

A comprehensive guide to the art of violin improvisation in jazz, blues, swing, folk, rock, and New Age. This book includes exercises, riffs, techniques, patterns, chord charts, tunes, photos, and quotes. Preface by Darol Anger. (Huiksi Music)

📖 *Rockin' Out with Blues Fiddle* by Julie Lyonn Lieberman

Rock and popular music developed from blues and R&B. This book is a comprehensive guide to playing the blues for bowed strings, complete with warm-ups, patterns, pentatonic scales, tunes, and historical information. Includes a practice CD. (Huiksi Music)

📖 *String Groove* by Edgar Gabriel

This book and companion CD offer twelve original tunes written by Edgar Gabriel in the styles of Irish fiddle, smooth jazz, jazz blues, rock, Middle Eastern, old-time fiddle, salsa, heavy-metal, Cajun fiddle, rock blues, swing jazz, and funk. *String Groove* is for violin students, teachers, and professionals who want to learn to improvise. Its techniques can also be applied to other musical instruments. (Opus Music Publishers)

🔊 Supplemental Discography: Popular Strings

Bond, *Shine* (Universal)

Deninzon, Joe, *Electric Blue* (Wilbers BluesRecords)

Mooke, Martha, *Enharmonic Vision* (Maximum Music Connections)

Rasputina, *Thanks for the Ether* (Sony)

Rasputina, *Transylvania Regurgitations* (Sony)

Rock and Roll Back-up (Homespun Tapes)

Vanessa-Mae, *Storm* (Virgin)

Vanessa-Mae, *The Violin Player* (Virgin)

Von Cello, *Breaking the Sound Barriers* (Von Cello)

Strings Around the World   7

A Brief Overview

From the Chinese *erhu* to the Swedish *nyckelharpa*, the Greek *lyra*, the Norwegian *Hardanger* fiddle, the Welsh *crwth*, the Brazilian *rebeca*, the Turkish and Iranian *kamancheh* (also spelled *kemanche*), the Cambodian *tro*, the Persian *rebaba*, the Apache *tsli'edo'a'tl*, the African *gonje*, the Middle Eastern *keman*, and the *vielle* from Occitan, bowed stringed instruments have assumed many physical forms in various world cultures throughout the centuries. The present Western European physical construct of the violin—the size and shape of the instrument and, of course, the design of the bow—is actually fairly recent within the lineage of bowed strings. Formalized in Italy in the sixteenth century, its present-day appearance has been accepted as the norm by many cultures, but not by all.

This chapter is in no way comprehensive, as each world style mentioned here could easily fill its own dedicated chapter or book. The goal is to provide a broad overview of the role of bowed strings in world music, as well as access to resources that can be used to pursue the style(s) of your choice.

Some traditions are not covered in this section. For instance, there are a number of fiddle styles in France, including the

The Gypsies of Pakistan, Iran, and Afghanistan play a bowed instrument that is somewhat larger than a violin and held vertically like a cello. Smaller cello-like instruments are used in Cambodian and Chinese music as well.

Breton music of Brittany. There is a Welsh fiddle tradition, and one from Newfoundland (the easternmost of Canada's provinces), as well as one from Persia. Violin has also gradually been integrated into Spanish flamenco music. The following sample discography can be used if you wish to pursue these styles.

Miscellaneous Support Materials: Strings Around the World

📖 *Fiddling Around the World* by Chris Haigh

This book describes fourteen fiddle styles from around the world and offers forty-eight original and traditional tunes to illustrate the styles. A bibliography of recordings and books relevant to each style is included. (Spartan Press)

📖 *Fiddling Around the World* by Mary Ann Harbar

Supported by a practice CD, this book offers folk music from North America, the British Isles, Western and Eastern Europe, and the Middle East. An excellent resource for exploring ethnic styles. (Mel Bay Publications)

📖 *Flamenco: Gypsy Dance and Music from Andalusia* edited by Claus Schreiner and translated by Mollie Comerford Peters

Written by a group of dedicated flamenco enthusiasts, this book traces the history and development of flamenco, the stirring form of folk dance created by the Gypsies of the Andalusian region of Spain in the nineteenth century and still popular today. (Amadeus Press)

📖 *Garland Encyclopedia of World Music*

Not specifically string-oriented, this book does present a wide overview of world music and, specifically, a number of fiddle styles. Includes photos and some notated examples. (Garland Publishing)

📖 *Music from the Heart* by Colin Quigley

This study of musical creativity in the aural tradition focuses on Emile Benoit (1913–1992), an exemplary traditional fiddler from French Newfoundland. *Music from the Heart* follows Benoit through a rapidly changing musical milieu, as he moves from a small rural community to international musical and folk festivals. (University of Georgia Press)

💿 Miscellaneous Discography: Strings Around the World

Breton: Christian Lemaitre with Kornog, *Ar Seizh Avel/On Seven Wings* (Green Linnet)

Breton: Christian Lemaitre with Kornog, *Kornog* (Green Linnet)

Cambodia: *Cambodge: Musique classique khmère, théâtre d'ombres et chants de mariage* (Inédit)

Cape Verde: Rufino Almeida, *Bau: Cape Verdean Melancholy* (Evolver)

Gypsy, flamenco, and jazz: Willie and Lobos, *Fandango Nights* (Rhino)

Gypsy, flamenco, and jazz: Willie and Lobos, *Gypsy Boogaloo* (Rhino)

Iran: The Kamkars, *The Kurdish Music of Iran*, (Kereshmeh)

Newfoundland: Rufus Guinchard, *Fathers of the Newfoundland Fiddle* (Pigeon Inlet Productions)

Spain: Milladoiro, *As Fadas de Estrano Nome* (SIF)

Welsh: The Kilbride Brothers, *Kilbride* (Fflach Tradd)

Welsh: Various artists, *Ffidil* (Flach Tradd)

Afro-Cuban

The melding of Spanish, French, and African cultures has produced a fertile musical environment in Cuba. *Son montuno* (also referred to as salsa, meaning "spicy"), *bolero*, *mambo*, *rumba*, *cha-cha-cha*, and *danzon* are all Cuban dances, each with its own specific musical accompaniment.

Jesus Florido

Cuban Americans, out of contact with their native island for many years, evolved the *charanga* band, consisting of one flute, two violins (most likely a leftover from the days when one acoustic violin couldn't be heard within a band), congas, timbales, piano, bass, and two or three singers.

The violinists in the band play melody, provide a rhythmic backdrop, and also have an opportunity to solo. The accompaniment for improvisation is called a *montuno,* which is a repeating rhythmic pattern, usually built over a I-IV-V chord progression. While there can be as many as ten layers of these rhythmic motifs sounded out simultaneously, each is built on an underlying rhythmic foundation called *clave.* There are two primary types of clave (see below).

Support Materials: Afro-Cuban

📖 *Latin Violin* by Sam Bardfeld

> This book provides a concise history of Cuban music and the violin's place in it. It also features transcriptions of the works of primary players in the genre. Includes a companion CD, a section on montunos, and a complete discography. (Gerard and Sarzin Publishing Co.)

💿 Discography: Afro-Cuban

Alvarez, Enrique, *Para Mi Santo* (Ahi-Nama)

Drenna, Eddie, *Lo Mejor de Tipica Novell* (Fania)

Fe, Alfredo de la, *Latitudes* (RykoLatino)

Fe, Alfredo de la, *Salsa Passion*, (Discos Fuentes)

Florido, Jesus, *Heading North* (Bee-Sharp)

Hanson, Susie, *The Salsa Never Ends* (Jazz Caliente)

Hanson, Susie, *Solo Flight* (Jazz Caliente)

Arabic

Before gaining popularity in Europe, bowed stringed instruments, such as the rebab, were integral to the music of the Arabs, Turks, and peoples of the Near East and North Africa. The European violin, introduced via Napoleon's campaigns, is known in the Arabic world as *keman*, or violin, and is used almost exclusively today. Moroccans play *gamba* style (on the knee), while Egyptians and Iranians hold the violin in the traditional European position under the chin. The Arabic tuning system is different from standard tuning, ranging from G, D, A, E (Moroccan) to G, D, A, D or A, E, A, E (Turkish) to G, D, G, D (Arabic). Iranian violinists have been known to use all three tuning systems.

In Arabic music, the *maqam* (mode) is the basis of all melodies and improvisations. There are thousands of maqam, and the placement of pitch is not based on the Western tempered system, which is built on equidistant half-steps, but rather a more complex tuning system, built on microtones that change depending upon the maqam in use.

The timbre of the instrument can range from a very rich Western classical tone to a more nasal, thin, penetrating tone, and the playing style tends to be highly ornamented, with slides, trills, and wide vibrato. Sometimes the player drones against an open string. Since the genre is overwhelmingly homophonic, melody and ornamentation are of primary importance to the music.

Support Materials: Arabic

📖 *The Music of the Arabs* by Habib Hassan Touma

Encompassing a history of more than 2,000 years, this book presents an overview of Arabic music throughout history and examines the artistic output of contemporary musicians, covering secular and sacred, instrumental and vocal, and improvised and composed music. Typical musical structures are elucidated, and a detailed bibliography and discography (mainly covering the last fifty years) are also provided. The paperback version includes an audio CD of seven traditional Arabic pieces performed by contemporary Arab musicians (Amadeus Press)

💿 Discography: Arabic

Lammam, George, *Planet Passion* (Ancient Future)

Mrad, Nidaa Abou, *Musique de la Nada* (Byblos)

Shaheen, Simon, with Soraya, *Desert Roses and Arabian Rhythms* (Ark)

Shaheen, Simon, and Qantara, *Blue Flame* (Ark)

Shaheen, Simon, *Turath* (Times Square)

Shawwa, Sami, *Master of the Arabic Violin* (Global Village Music)

Classical Music of Iran: Dastgah Systems (Smithsonian Folkways)

The Music of Upper and Lower Egypt (Rykodisc)

Mystic Fiddle of the Proto-Gypsies (Shanachie)

Taqasim: Improvisation in Arabic Music (Lyrichord)

Asian

It is believed that the concept for the bow originated in Asia. The bowed instruments in that region are generally two- or three-stringed, and notes are played by placing the fingernail on the side of the string rather than by using downward pressure.

In China, one can find the *matouqin* (a cello-like two-stringed Mongolian upright fiddle) and the *huqin* (a small, vertically played two-stringed violin). The Chinese *erhu* (also played vertically) and the *jinhu* (a slightly smaller instrument) are also two-stringed fiddles. These instruments are used in the Peking Opera, a Chinese art form that combines music, acrobatics, masks, and stylized acting. In addition, the *banhu*, which is of northern origin, and the *gaohu* from the south are both two-stringed, vertically played instruments.

In Cambodia, the *tro*, a two-stringed fiddle, is used in the traditional Cambodian orchestra, which consists of two *roneat* (bamboo xylophones), various drums, *ghong* (small, tuned gongs) and a *srlay* (an oboe-like woodwind).

There are three sizes: the *tro u* and the larger *tro so* have two strings each, and the *tro khmer*, the largest of the three, has three strings.

Both the Cambodian tro and the Chinese erhu are held on the knee in European cello position. The player uses both sides of the bow-hair as the bow moves between the strings, pushing down for the low pitches and pulling up for the high ones.

All of these instruments are tuned in fifths. Since none have fingerboards, the player is able to create highly expressive sounds by ornamenting the melody with slides, grace notes, and warbles, in conjunction with a wide variety of bowed dynamics.

💿 Discography: Asian

Cambodian: *The Music of Cambodia* (Celestial Harmonies)

Chinese: Liu Ming-Yuan, *Favorite Huqin Pieces* (Hugo)

Chinese: *Chinese Traditional Erhu Music* (Oliver Sudden Productions)

Chinese: Zhou Yu, *The Art of the Chinese Erhu* (Arc Music)

Mongolian: Darima Qinggele and Aotegeng Bayar, *Matouqin* (Hugo)

Brazilian

There are no well-known string players associated exclusively with Brazilian music, but violinist Raimundo Nilton has been developing the field, both as a player and an educator. The world recognizes bossa nova as the primary style of Brazil. Bossa nova has become so integral to jazz in the United States that it is an essential component of any jazz player's repertoire. The most popular tunes are those composed by Antonio Carlos Jobim. Most bossas are thirty-two bars in length, and the melody leads into improvisation on chord changes, just as it does in jazz standards.

With the extensive popularity of bossa nova worldwide, other styles from Brazil have been overlooked, such as *xote, baião, frevo* (all from the northeast of Brazil), *choro,* and *samba.* These styles do not include European classical violin, although a handful of American violinists have included them in their repertoire. The bowed string instrument that is a part of Brazilian culture is the *rebeca*: a rustic, handmade fiddle played at fairs in the Brazilian countryside. It is held against the left breast rather than on the shoulder, to facilitate singing while playing. Rebeca performers traditionally improvise song/stories and use a lot of grace notes in the ornamentation.

Baião (2/4 meter) and *xote* (4/4) are both dance styles. They originated at countryside dances but are now popular throughout Brazil. These styles consist of popular songs about love, dance, and sexuality with syncopated melodies.

Frevo and *choro* are very fast instrumental music styles consisting mostly of straight eighth-notes. Frevo is specifically from the town of Recife and is played at parties during Carnival. Frevo bands consist mostly of brass and percussion. Choro is from Rio de Janeiro and is more for listening than for the dancing and drinking associated with frevo music.

Instrumentation for choro music consists of solo instruments (mandolin or *cavaquinho,* a plucked lute with characteristics of both a guitar and mandolin) accompanied by seven-string guitar and mandolin. The only percussion used is a *pandeiro* (a tamborine with complicated rhythm patterns). Sometimes a large *surdo* drum is played as well.

Support Materials: Brazilian

 Volume 31: Bossa Novas

It has become standard practice today for professional musicians to play at least one Latin tune per set as added spice to their overall sound. This play-along CD contains ten beautiful bossa nova standards, complete with melody, chords, and lyrics. Includes transposed parts. (Jamey Aebersold Jazz)

🎵 Discography: Brazilian

Nilton, Raimundo, *Violinando* (Valores da Terra)

Turtle Island String Quartert, with Caito Marcondes, *Porta do Templo* (CPC Umes)

Canadian (Cape Breton, Cree, Métis, Québécois)

Canadian fiddle styles include Cape Breton, Québécois or French-Canadian, Cree, Métis, Acadian, Prince Edward Island, Ontario-style, and more. A parallel can be drawn between the United States and Canada, in that the original indigenous peoples of both countries created vocal music accompanied by drum, and in some cases, wooden flute. The fiddle was introduced via Celtic fiddle music, which came to Canada with the Scottish, Irish, and French. Regional "accents," as well as degrees of intermingling, were determined by who settled where. For instance, Cape Breton music has a strong

Natalie MacMaster

Scottish influence, whereas Prince Edward Island consists of a mixture of Irish, Scottish, and French traditions. Québéc is heavily French-influenced, but some of its top fiddlers, including Jean Carignan, listened to and played everything, and many Québécois had Irish ancestry. The Irish tunes in Québécois music are played with a French feel.

The term *traditional* describes the older tunes for which there are no known composers. These tunes have been handed down aurally for centuries, and most maintain the same thirty-two bar AABB structure, consisting of two eight-bar melodic phrases. Meters include 3/4, 4/4, 6/8, and 9/8. Traditional repertoire is made up of dance music, including jigs, reels, waltzes, slow aires, hornpipes, and, in some areas, clog dances. Region-to-region distinctions can be found in ornamentation and bowing styles, as well as some variations in rhythmic phrasing. For instance, the Métis often play tunes in irregular meter.

Métis is a western Canadian fiddle style that can be traced back to the French and Scottish traders who sailed into northern Canada in the late 1600s and subsequently brought their fiddle styles to western Canada during the early days of the fur trade. The Métis are the descendants of a mixture of European and aboriginal blood. The Métis repertoire consists of dance tunes that include well-known Scottish fiddle pieces such as "Whiskey Before Breakfast," as well as tunes developed by the Métis.

Métis fur traders brought fiddle music to the Cree hunters of James Bay. The Cree repertoire consists of fiddle tunes handed down within the Cree tribe that can be traced all of the way back to tunes brought from the British Isles. All of the tunes are associated with specific dances.

Both French Canadian and Cape Breton fiddling tend to feature staccato use of the bow and, in some cases, flying spiccato at dazzling tempos.

Support Materials: Canadian

📖 *Canadian Fiddle Music* compiled by Dr. Ed Whitcomb

This book features transcriptions of tunes from every province and ethnic group in Canada. (Mel Bay Publications)

📖 *Brenda Stubbert's Collection of Fiddle Tunes*

This collection focuses on contemporary performers and the continuing musical tradition in Cape Breton, Nova Scotia. It contains both traditional and newly composed tunes from Cape Breton, Scottish, Irish, and other sources, transcribed as played by featured performers. A significant number of the melodies are compositions by Jerry Holland and Brenda Stubbert, as both are prolific composers of new tunes in the style. (Cranford Publications)

📖 *Jerry Holland's Collection*

A healthy balance of Irish and Scottish traditional standards and contemporary Cape Breton compositions are featured in this book. (Cranford Publications)

💿 Discography: Canadian

Canadian: Frederick "Ned" Landry, *International Fiddling Champion* (Atlantica)

Canadian: Anne Lederman, *Seven Cats* (Falcon Productions)

Canadian: Don Messer, *Don Messer's Violin* (TRDC)

Cape Breton: Joe Cormier, *The Dances Down Home* (Rounder)

Cape Breton: Jerry Holland, *Master Cape Breton Fiddler* (Fiddlesticks Music)

Cape Breton: Dave MacIsaac, *From the Archives* (Pickin' Productions)

Cape Breton: Donald MacLellan, *The Dusky Meadow* (Rounder)

Cape Breton: Buddy MacMaster, *The Judique Flyer* (Stephen MacDonald Productions)

Cape Breton: Buddy MacMaster, *Cape Breton Tradition* (Rounder)

Cape Breton: Natalie MacMaster, *Natalie MacMaster Live* (Rounder)

Cape Breton: Natalie MacMaster, *My Roots Are Showing* (MacMaster Music)

Cape Breton: Brenda Stubbert, *Music All Around* (Cranford Publications)

Cree: James Cheechoo, *Shay Chee Man* (Kwiskhegun Productions)

Cree: James Cheechoo, *Neemitdau* (Kwiskhegun Productions)

Métis: John Arcand, *The Tunes of the Red River* (e-mail: windy.acres@sasktel.net)

Métis: John Arcand, *Traditionally Yours* (e-mail: windy.acres@sasktel.net)

Métis: Calvin Vollrath, *Fiddillennium* (Spirit River)

Métis: Calvin Vollrath, *Métis Old Time Dance Tunes* (Spirit River)

Métis: *Old Native and Métis Fiddling in Manitoba* (Falcon Productions)

Métis and Turtle Island: *Turtle Mountain Music* (Folkways)

Ontario: Peter Dawson, *Owl in the Henhouse* (Peter Dawson Violins)

Prince Edward Island: Albert Arsenault, *Barachois Naturel* (House Party Productions)

Québécois: Jean Carignan, *Homage à Joseph Allard* (Rounder)

Québécois: Jean Carignan, *Jean Carignan* (Rounder)

Québécois: Jean Carignan, *Coleman, Morrison, & Skinner* (Rounder)

Québécois: Yvon Cuillerier, *Québéc–Pure Laine* (Tb-049-Cas)

Québécois: Yvon Cuillerier, *Violin De Chez-Nous* (L'association Québécoise des loisirs folkloriques)

Québécois: Louis "Pitou" Boudreault, *Musique Traditionelle du Québéc* (Tamanoir)

Québécois: Louis Boudreault, *Old Time Fiddler of Chicoutimi, Quebec* (Voyager)

Québécois: Joe Bouchard, *Musique Traditionelle du Québéc* (Tamanoir)

Celtic (Irish, Scottish, and Shetland Island)

The term *Celtic music* has become a catch phrase. In general, it refers to the traditional music of the Celtic countries: Ireland, Scotland, Wales, Brittany (in France), and Galicia (in Spain). The Celts as an identifiable race are long gone, and there are strong differences between the traditional music of each Celtic country. It is interesting to find that the term *Celtic* is actually used the most in the United States and Canada, where the tradition is much more diverse in terms of mixtures of styles—from traditional to variations such as Afro-Celtic, Galician Celtic (the music of northwestern Spain), or New Age contemporary Celtic (as in the artist Enya). Here we will focus on the traditional aspects of the music.

The Celtic people date back over two thousand years. Their music as we know it today has been handed down for over four hundred years, passed aurally from generation to generation. Most tunes are without known composers and are therefore called traditional. However, there are two composers of particular note still played today: the Irish harpist Turlough O'Carolan (1670–1738), whose tunes were adapted to fiddle, and the Scottish fiddler and composer James Scott Skinner (1843–1927), dubbed "the Strathspey King," due to the large number of strathspeys he composed. (A strathpey is a Scottish dance in 4/4 with a proclivity for dotted eighth-notes.)

Scottish fiddling is distinguished by its dotted rhythms and staccato bow style. Irish music lilts and tends to use more slurs. Most Celtic tunes are thirty-two bars in length, built on an AABB structure made up of repeated eight-bar melodic phrases. Meters include 3/4, 4/4, 6/8, and 9/8. Celtic repertoire is made up of dance music, including jigs, reels, waltzes, slow aires, strathspeys, and hornpipes. Regional distinctions lie in the ornamentation and bowing styles. The Celtic repertoire includes so many thousands of tunes and subsequent variations (with new names) that no two fiddlers from different regions are likely to share more than a dozen tunes in common.

Due to its geographic placement, the music of the Shetland Islands has been influenced by both Norwegian and Scottish music. Despite increasing Scottish influence on the Nordic culture of the Shetlands, the Island fiddling has remained remarkably distinctive. While many tunes do have Scottish roots, there are over one hundred that cannot be traced to Scottish ancestry. Rather, they have a distinctive "Shetland feel" about them. These are mostly reels, for up until the early years of the present century, the reel was, for the most part, the only dance performed. The Shetland repertoire of reels only began to be supplemented with polkas, quadrilles, and other Scottish country dances after World War I.

It is common for fiddlers in the Celtic traditions to gather regularly in music sessions called *ceilidhs*. Tunes, each of which may be repeated a number of times, are usually grouped together in medleys. Fiddlers often take turns leading.

Irish music is so popular in America that it could have just as easily been included in the chapter, "American Fiddle Styles."

Live shows such as *Riverdance,* which has been aired on television, as well as the massive popularity of singer Enya and groups including the Chieftans, have helped familiarize the public with this richly inspiring genre. Try to expose your students to traditional Irish players, such as Michael Coleman or Tommy Peoples, so that they understand the origin of the more contemporary players.

Support Materials: Celtic

📖 *Canadian Old-Time Fiddle Hits, Volumes I and II* by Gordon Stobbe

This anthology of classic old-time fiddle tunes has been culled from cross-Canada jam-session lists compiled by fiddlers, accompanists, and fans. The collection contains seventy standards, including regional favorites from western Canada, the Ottawa Valley, Québéc, and the Maritimes.

The book is available with or without a companion CD. The CD is also available in a separate jewel case. (New Traditions)

📖 *English, Welsh, Scottish, and Irish Fiddle Tunes* by Robin Williamson

The tunes in this book are mostly obscure, and it is therefore not particularly useful as a teaching tool for those new to Celtic music sessions. However, it does have great personality and is much more interesting than other more sterile, mass-produced collections. Specifically, Williamson teaches basic ornamentation and presents a paragraph of information on each tune. Includes a companion CD. (Music Sales Corp.)

📖 *Fifty Fiddle Solos* by Aly Bain

This book contains transcriptions of fifty Shetland Island fiddle tunes. Renowned Shetland Island fiddler Aly Bain demonstrates on a companion CD with full accompaniment. (Music Sales Corp.)

📖 *The Glen Collection of Scottish Dance Music*

Transcriptions of nearly three hundred unique strathspeys and reels from the John Glen collection (1891 and 1895) are presented in this book. Ornamentation symbols are not included. (Highland Music Trust)

📖 *Kindred Spirits: A Musical Portrait of Scotland's Women* by Bonnie Rideout

This book contains note-for-note transcriptions of the selections featured on Rideout's popular CD of the same title. It is a collection of solo, twin, and triple fiddle tunes, honoring the contribution women have made to Scots culture. (Mel Bay Publications)

📖 *Learn to Play Irish Fiddle* with Kevin Burke

Master fiddler Burke covers the basics of true Irish fiddle style on video. He teaches the melody of each tune and then presents nuances that make the music come alive. (Homespun Tapes)

📖 *Scottish Fire: Traditional and Original Tunes for Fiddle from 1762 to the Present* by Bonnie Rideout

This collection presents favorite tunes that Rideout had stashed away over the years while awaiting the perfect opportunity to record them. J. Scott Skinner tunes are included. The package includes a book and a CD. (Mel Bay Publications)

📖 *Under the Moon: Thirteen Celtic Solos* by Martin Hayes

This book presents thirteen transcriptions of tunes as interpreted by Martin Hayes, complete with notations for cuts, rolls, and other bow movements. (Mel Bay Publications)

💿 Discography: Celtic

Celtic/Galician: Milladoiro, *As Fadas de Estraño Nome* (Green Linnet)

Celtic/Galician: Carlos Nuñez, *Brotherhood of Stars* (RCA)

Irish: *An Historic Recording of Irish Traditional Music from County Clare and East Galway* (Shanachie)

Irish: *Traditional Irish Music in America* (Rounder)

Irish: Boys of the Lough, *Farewell and Remember Me* (Shenachie)

Irish meets Breton: Kevin Burke, Johnny Cunningham, and Christian Lemaître, *Rendezvous* (Green Linnet)

Irish: Kevin Burke, *Kevin Burke in Concert* (Green Linnet)

Irish: Liz Carroll, *Lake Effect* (Green Linnet)

Irish: Liz Carroll, *Lost in the Loop* (Green Linnet)

Irish: The Chieftans, *Best of the Chieftans* (Sony)

Irish: Michael Coleman, *Michael Coleman 1891 to 1945* (Gael Linn)

Irish: Séamus Connelly, *Notes from my Mind* (Green Linnet)

Irish: Séamus Connelly, *Warming Up* (Green Linnet)

Irish: Brian Conway, *First Through the Gate* (Smithsonian Folkways)

Irish: Martin Hayes, *Under the Moon* (Green Linnet)

Irish: Martin Hayes, *Live in Seattle* (Green Linnet)

Irish: Patrick Ourceau, *Tracin': Traditional Music from the West of Ireland* (Celtic Crossings)

Irish: Tommy Peoples, *Waiting for a Call* (Shanachie)

Scottish: Alasdair Fraser, *Legacy of the Scottish Fiddle* (Culburnie)

Scottish: Iain Fraser, *Touchwood* (Capontree Music)

Scottish: Bonnie Rideout, *Scottish Inheritance* (The Orchard)

Scottish: Bonnie Rideout, *Scottish Fire* (Maggie's Music)

Scottish: *Scottish Traditional Fiddle* (Legacy)

Shetland Islands: Aly Bain and Phil Cunningham, *Another Gem* (COM)

Shetland Islands and Scandinavian: Aly Bain and Ale Möller, *Fully Rigged* (North)

Eastern European and Russian

It is surprising to find that the musicians of the Eastern European countries have maintained clearly defined regional styles, even though the borders between these countries have shifted so many times over the centuries. There are folk tunes identified as coming from Romania, Russia, the Ukraine, Poland, Hungary,

Moldavia, Latvia, Estonia, Transylvania, Czechoslovakia (now the Czech Republic and Slovakia), Serbia, and Croatia. Many of these tunes are integral to specific dances and celebrations. Eastern European and Russian musicians must have enormous stamina, as a single dance—within a whole evening of dances—can be played for as long as ninety minutes. There is a particular wealth of wedding songs, because a traditional wedding in these regions can last for more than two days and features non-stop music.

The *csárdá*, a dance tune, is a popular music form. The word itself means "a village inn." There are thousands of czardas (pub dances). Other regional forms include *kolmyjkas*, *shers*, polkas, and waltzes.

It should be noted that the viola plays a prominent role in some Eastern European music. In the music of Transylvania, the viola has three strings (G, D, and A). The A string is an octave lower than normal classical tuning. The bridge is almost flat, enabling the player to sound out chords and, together with the bass player, provide rhythm.

Support Materials: Eastern European and Russian

Eastern European Music for Violin Duets by Mary Ann Harbar

This book features transcriptions of ninety-two Eastern European folk melodies. Includes a companion split-track CD. (Mel Bay Publications)

How to Play Romanian Folk Violin by Miamon Miller

This book contains more than thirty pages of background information, transcriptions, maps, and drawings. The ten notated folk-dance pieces are accompanied by a stereo cassette on which both the melodic line and the style of playing back-up are illustrated. (Elderly Books)

📖 *How to Play Romanian Folk Violin, Vol. 2* by Miamon Miller and Larche Cerael

This book and companion cassette explore twelve pieces of Romanian music. Techniques and stylistic nuances are presented with regional variations of accordion, guitar, and violin accompaniment. (Elderly Books)

💿 Discography: Eastern European and Russian

Eastern European: Chris Haigh, with Tziganarama, *Tree of Life* (website: www.fiddlingaround.co.uk)

Eastern European: *Unblocked: Music of Eastern Europe* (Ellipsis Arts)

Eastern European: *Rough Guide: The Music of Eastern Europe* (World Music Network)

Hungarian: *Eastern Europe* (World Music Network)

Hungarian: *Hungarian Music from Transylvania: Folk Traditions from Gyimes and the Great Plain* (Inedit)

Hungarian: *May I Kiss Your Hand: Hungarian & Gypsy Fiddle Music & Songs* (Arhoolie)

Polish: *Fire in the Mountains: Polish Mountain Fiddle Music* (Yazoo)

Ukrainian: *Ukrainian Village Music* (Arhoolie)

Transylvanian: *Transilvania Express* (cdRoots)

Greek

Since well before the seventeenth century, the pear-shaped *lyra* was the primary bowed string instrument in Greek music. The lyra has three strings (A, D, G) and is played like the Chinese *erhu*: in cello position, rested against one knee. It is fingered by touching the nail to the side of the string, rather than by pressing down from above. Between 1850 and 1950, the lyra was replaced throughout most of Greece by the modern violin.

As is the case with so many fiddle styles worldwide, Greek violin is intricately intertwined with dance, and every dance has a purpose, a history, and a context. Greek violin is also associated with vocal music. Songs in the current Greek repertoire date back as far as the thirteenth century. There are many regional styles—from mountain music to urban. The latter includes *rembetika* (urban blues Greek-style) and *smyrneika* (a cabaret tradition from the town of Smyrna that reflects the musical influence of its Turkish, Armenian, and Jewish populations). Each village has its own rhythms, songs, and dances.

It is not uncommon in Greek music to see a key signature that contains a sharp and a flat simultaneously or a time signature in 7/8. Some scales contain notes outside the parameters of Western tempered intonation. Quarter-tones are used (pitches located halfway between two tempered notes). Some songs are built on pentatonic (five-note) scales and others on *makam,* or *maqam* (modes), roughly three hundred of which were brought over by Greeks from Turkey in the 1920s.

The violin is often used to create a drone by sounding the melody against an open string, and the bow is moved in a driving rhythm to help support the dancers. In most cases, improvisation is integral to the music.

💿 Discography: Greek

Chalkias, Achileas, *Petro-Loukas Chalkias & Kompani* (World Network)

Cohen, Beth, *Weaving the Worlds* (Beth Bahia Cohen)

Gouventas, Kyriakos, with Savina Yannatou, *Terra Nostra* (ECM)

Kalaintzis, Nikos, with Nikos Moraitis and Kyriakos Gouventas,
    "Angelo," *The Greek Folk Instruments Vol. 5, The Violin* (F.M.)

Folk Music of Greece and Cyprus (Lyrichord Discs)

Gypsy

Historians believe that the Roma people—more commonly known as the Gypsies—first came from northern India in the eleventh century AD. Migration moved them first through Persia, Armenia, Greece, the Balkans, and Rumania, followed by the movement of splinter groups into Eastern and Western Europe and beyond.

Although they were outcasts wherever they went, Gypsies also had a reputation as skilled musicians. They would learn the local music and play at dances, weddings, and other social events. Interestingly, there was also a rich exchange between Gypsy and klezmer musicians, since both groups were ostracized throughout Europe and thus came to turn to one another for help.

A good deal of the regional music Gypsies learned was traditional, meaning without a known composer. This music was never notated; rather, it has been passed aurally from person to person, violin to violin. The Gypsies also performed their own vocal music accompanied by hand percussion. Improvisation plays an important role in Gypsy performance.

Gypsy violin is known for its strenuous technical requirements, use of *glissandi*, full-throttle vibrato, and Olympian tempos. The music is full of passion, with changes in tempo and some non-Western scales.

Support Materials: Gypsy

🎬 *Carpati* directed by Yale Strom

This film (available on VHS) explores Jewish and Gypsy cultural inter-relationships through music in the Carpathian mountains of the Ukraine. (New Yorker Films)

📖 *The Gypsy Fiddler* selected and arranged by Edward Huws Jones

This book features transcriptions of fifteen fiddle tunes with piano accompaniments from Hungary, Transylvania, and Romania. Includes five popular Gypsy tunes. (Boosey and Hawkes)

📖 *Gypsy Violin* by Mary Ann Harbar

Based on many years of research and travel, this book contains practice tips, a short essay on the Gypsy touch, and a fine assortment of approximately fifty annotated traditional Gypsy tunes from

Russia, Romania, Hungary, and Bessarabia. Includes a helpful glossary. (Mel Bay Publications)

🎞 *Latcho Drom* directed by Tony Gatlif

In Romany, *latcho drom* means "safe journey." Available on VHS and DVD, this haunting, vibrant, award-winning film is neither a documentary nor fiction but a musical that tells the story of the historic odyssey of the Gypsies from India to Egypt and depicts the pain and joy of being an outsider. Features Gypsy musicians from India, Egypt, Turkey, Romania, Hungary, Slovakia, France, and Spain. Romany with English subtitles. (New Yorker Films)

📖 *Uncertain Roads: Searching for the Gypsies* by Yale Strom

This book focuses on Rom history and contemporary life. Strom offers historical summaries, interviews, and photographs. Urban and rural populations in Romania, Hungary, Ukraine, and Sweden are described, and first-person narratives from a variety of Rom men, women, and children are included. Each chapter concludes with a musical score, with lyrics in Romani and English. (Simon and Schuster)

💿 Discography: Gypsy

Band of Gypsies (Atlantic)
The Fortuneteller (Arklow)
Gypsy Blues (Loyko)
Gypsy Time for Nuniya (Network Medien)
Loyko in Russia (Boheme Music)
Master of Rumanian Fiddle (Auvidis)
Return of Gypsy Maestro (Loyko)
Road of the Gypsies (Network Medien)
Rough Guide: Music of the Gypsies (World Music Network)
Taraf de Haidouks (Nonesuch)

Indian (North and South)

The basis for Indian music is *sangeet*. Sangeet is a combination of three art forms: vocal music, instrumental music, and dance. There are two systems of Indian music: the South Indian (*Carnatic)* sangeet style and the North Indian (*Hindustani)* sangeet style. Both musical systems are built on *raga* and *tala*. Raga is the melodic form while tala is the rhythmic. North and South Indian music also have distinct musical differences, but these are too detailed to explore here.

Carnatic Violin

The Indian violin is identical in form to the Western violin, but its tuning is different, as is its playing position. The Indian violin is an important solo instrument, and, in South Indian music, it often accompanies a vocal performance.

According to most accounts, the earliest master musicians to successfully adapt the violin to Carnatic music were Balasvamy Diksitar (1786–1858) and Vadivelu (1810–1845). Both men studied the Western style of violin playing before going on to experiment with their own music. Some Indian players have experimented with left-hand techniques in an effort to emulate the singer's vocal ornaments—particularly the slide techniques—by using two fingers instead of four. The smooth transition between the two fingers is accomplished by a rolling motion of the wrist. It is the same motion through which, in Western technique, vibrato is practiced. Since the exclusive use of this technique limits the smooth execution of melodic lines, a left-hand technique gradually evolved to accommodate both the need for intricately timed slides and the ability to run clusters of notes.

The Carnatic violinist sits cross-legged, bracing the instrument lightly between the collarbone and the hollow of the right ankle, where the scroll of the violin rests. This frees the performer's left hand to play Indian ornamentation, called *gamaka*, which include a series of intricately timed slides; broad *kampitas* (oscillations); and rolls.

Hindustani Violin

The violin traveled from the south to the north. It took longer to gain acceptance in the north because the *sarangi* was in use. The sarangi is an Indian violin that has three or four primary strings and up to three dozen sympathetic strings. The instrument has no frets or fingerboard; the strings are suspended. Pitch is determined by sliding the fingernail against the string rather than pressing it against a fingerboard, and the sarangi is held in cello position.

Today there are far fewer violinists in the north than in the south. During the Persian invasions of India (the *Mughal* period beginning around the thirteenth century), Persian music was introduced and blended with current Hindustani musical forms. The south did not have that evolution. South Indian music is very stylized and has a rigid formal structure. North Indian music has open boundaries that allow for extensive improvisation. Other dissimilarities include how each system counts beats and maintains rhythmic cycles.

Support Materials: Indian

📖 *The Raga Guide: A Survey of 74 Hindustani Ragas*

This important book offers a wonderful introduction to ragas, with both Western and Indian notation and examples on four companion CDs. (Nimbus)

💿 Discography: Indian

Indian and Pakistani: *The Rough Guide to the Music of India and Pakistan* (World Music Network)

South Indian: Lalgudi Jayaraman, *Live Concert at Sri Krishna* (EMI India)

South Indian: Lalgudi Jayaraman, *Violin Virtuoso* (Oriental)

South Indian: L. Shankar and V. Lakshminarayana, *Nobody Told Me* (ECM)

South Indian: L. Subramaniam, *Indian Classical Masters: Three Ragas for Solo Violin* (Nimbus)

North and South Indian: M. S. Gopalakrishnan, *Live at Narada Gana Sabha Chennai, Vol. 1* (EMI India)

North Indian: Dr. N. Rajam, *The Enchanting Violin of Dr. N. Rajam* (Oriental)

North Indian: Dr. N. Rajam, *The Vibrant Violin of Dr. N. Rajam* (Oriental)

Fusion: Vicki Richards, *Parting the Waters* (Third Stream Music)

Fusion: Vicki Richards, *Quiet Touch* (New Age)

Fusion: Vicki Richards, *Live in India* (New Age)

Klezmer

The term *klezmer* originally came from two Hebrew words—*kley* and *zemer*—which referred to musical instruments. In Yiddish, klezmer means "musician," while in English, the word now refers to the musical genre as a whole. The early *klezmorim* (Jewish musicians) played primarily for Jewish weddings and sometimes for other Jewish events. Attitudes towards the Jews throughout Europe affected when and where they could work in all fields, so only at certain times and in certain places were they hired for non-Jewish events.

Mutual support between the Jews and the Gypsies—both persecuted groups—as well as constant relocation of the Jews throughout Central and Eastern Europe over the centuries, exposed klezmer musicians to Middle Eastern music and the folk musics of Eastern Europe: Romanian, Polish, Russian Gypsy, Ukrainian, and Hungarian.

Violin was the primary instrument in klezmer bands until the late 1800s, when clarinet took its place as the lead instrument. Recordings of Jewish music made in America between 1912 and 1940 created a rich resource that led to the revival of klezmer music in the 1970s. The modern klezmer band consists of at least one singer, violin and clarinet (or mixed woodwinds), and a range of traditional and nontraditional instruments, depending upon the group concept.

Violinists ornament klezmer music with slides, bends, and pin-kied grace notes (called *krechz*) that interact with each other in split-second timing, creating a vocal sound akin to keening, wailing, or moaning. Yet the music is upbeat and celebratory. It is as if klezmer music speaks to the listener, "No matter how hard life is, I will express it *and* celebrate all that is good." Some pieces change tempo, and most are built on scales that contain at least one gap of a minor third, as opposed to the Western diatonic scale that is built on half and whole steps.

Support Materials: Klezmer

📖 *The Book of Klezmer: The History, the Music, the Folklore* by Yale Strom

This book covers klezmer history and music from the fourteenth through the twenty-first century. It includes photos, interviews, and a glossary. (A Cappella Books)

📼 *Carpati* directed by Yale Strom

This film (available on VHS) explores Jewish and Gypsy cultural inter-relationships through music in the Carpathian mountains of the Ukraine. (New Yorker Films)

📖 *The Klezmer Collection* by Stacy Phillips

This book offers a collection of 120 melodies meticulously tran-scribed from recordings by masters of the klezmer style, including Dave Tarras, Naftule Brandwine, Abe Schwartz, and many more. Written in standard notation for C instruments, it includes chordal accompaniments. (Mel Bay Publications)

📖 *The Compleat Klezmer* by Henry Sapoznik

This book represents the first complete history of klezmer music. Beginning with its origins in early-nineteenth-century Poland, Sapoznik tracks klezmer's musical and cultural history in nine-teenth-century Europe and twentieth-century America. Sapoznik highlights the contributions of such prominent musicians as George Gershwin, Paul Robeson, and Itzhak Perlman, all of whom had ties to klezmer. (Tara)

📼 *The Last Klezmer* directed by Yale Strom

As seen through the eyes of klezmer musician, photographer, and filmmaker Yale Strom, *The Last Klezmer* (available on VHS) portrays the animated life and music of Leopold Kozlowski, the last known performing klezmer musician to have grown up in Poland with this rich musical tradition. Strom retraces Kozlowski's life through memory, music, and a journey back to his hometown of Przemyslany (near Lvov, Ukraine). We see Kozlowski today as a conductor and music teacher, passing his knowledge of Jewish music to a new generation of Catholic Poles. (distributed by Artistic License)

📖 *The Klezmer Fiddler* selected and arranged by Edward Huws Jones

This book features sixteen popular klezmer tunes with piano accompaniment. (Boosey and Hawkes)

📖 *World Music: Klezmer* by Yale Strom

This book opens with a historical introduction and then presents transcriptions of five klezmer tunes. A play-along CD is included. (Universal Edition)

💿 Discography: Klezmer

Haigh, Chris, *The Angels Sing Klezmania* (website: www.fiddlingaround.co.uk)

Strom, Yale, *Hot Pstromi: With a Little Horseradish on the Side* (Global Village Music)

Strom, Yale, *Carpati: 50 Miles* (Global Village Music)

Strom, Yale, *Tales Our Fathers Sang: New Jewish Music with Tam* (Global Village Music)

Svigals, Alicia, *Fidl* (Traditional Crossroads)

Svigals, Alicia, *Possessed* (Xenophile)

Khevrisa: European Klezmer Music (Smithsonian Folkways)

The Klezmatics, *Rhythm and Jews* (Xenophile)

The Klezmatics, *Jews with Horns* (Xenophile)

Klezmer Music 1910–1942 (Global Village)

A Marriage of Heaven and Earth (Ellipsis Arts)

The Rough Guide to Klezmer (World Music Network)

Mexican

In the United States, earlier versions of the fiddle—the three-stringed, foot-long *rabel* and other small fiddles from sixteenth- and seventeenth-century Europe—were replaced by the symphonic violin by the late eighteenth century. This total conversion did not occur in Mexico, where the rabel, renamed *raweali* or *raweri*, continues to be built and played as well as the European violin.

Juan Reynoso (L) with Paul Anastasio (R)

Fiddle is extremely popular in Mexican music. It can be found throughout the country. The Huichol people of western Mexico and the Chamulas of southern Mexico are both examples of cultures in which the fiddle is central to spiritual ritual. Other indigenous communities, such as the Rarámuris, Huastecan, Nahua, Tarahumara, and Tzotzil, use their fiddle music to accompany dance, spiritual ceremonies, and social events.

The evolution of fiddle music in Mexico is similar to that in the United States and Canada. Throughout North America, the fiddle was introduced by conquerors (in Mexico's case, the Spanish) or immigrants, and fiddle styles evolved regionally based on geography, history, and local customs.

The two best-known Mexican fiddle genres are *Calentana* and *Jalisco*. The former is the music of the Mexican Hotlands, kept alive largely through the efforts of American fiddler Paul

Anastasio. The latter, which is now known as mariachi, has become extremely popular in the United States and is played by dozens of high school mariachi fiddle clubs and orchestras.

Calentana groups usually consist of two fiddles, one or two guitars, and a *tamborita* (a small wooden drum). The traditional Jalisco ensemble consisted of two violins, a large harp, a *vihuela* (small guitar), and a *quinta de golpe* (a larger guitar-like instrument). Ultimately, the bass guitar replaced the harp in mariachi music, and, when trumpet replaced first violin, the violin section had to be increased in size to compete with the volume of the horn. Traditional mariachi repertoire includes the *son jaliscience* and the *jarabe*.

Support Materials: Mexican

☐ *Mariachi Violin Transcriptions* arranged by Laura Sobrino

A collection of transcriptions written for the "non-mariachi musician," this book has ten traditional mariachi tunes written for one to two violins, guitar, and bass. The violin parts pull out for easy reading, and the score includes both rhythmic/chord notation for a guitar and notation for a bass instrument. (Mel Bay Publications)

☐ *Hal Leonard Mariachi Series*

Each arrangement includes a professionally recorded demonstration on its companion CD. The pieces have been scored for violins, trumpets, armonia, guitarron, and vocals. Instrumentation options are available for flute, guitar, and bass. (Hal Leonard)

💿 Discography: Mexican

Calentana: Juan Reynoso with Neyo and Javier Reynoso, *On Fire and In Concert* (Swing Cat Enterprises)

Calentana: Juan Reynoso with Neyo and Javier Reynoso, *Hot as Habanero* (Swing Cat Enterprises)

Calentana: Juan Reynoso with Neyo and Javier Reynoso, *Viva Tierra Caliente* (Swing Cat Enterprises)

Calentana: Juan Reynoso with Neyo and Javier Reynoso, *With Passion* (Swing Cat Enterprises)

Mariachi: *All the Best from Mexico: 40 Mexican Favorites* [2-CD Set] (Madacy)

Mariachi: *Mariachi from Mexico* (Delta)

Native American

Singing has traditionally been the primary musical form among Native American tribes. When it comes to instruments, drums, rattles, and flutes have typically been the most common, but certain tribal nations have integrated the violin into their music as well. Some groups used the fiddle to play the melodies of the old songs, while others learned new fiddle tunes from their Scottish, French, and Irish neighbors.

The Apache people of Arizona and Inuit of the Arctic continue to build their own type of fiddle. It is believed that both nations were inspired by the violins carried by European settlers and sailors. The Apache fiddle has one string on it and is carved from the stalk of the agave plant. It has been a part of tribal music for over one hundred years. The Apaches call theirs *tsli'edo'a'tl*, meaning "wood that sings." It is also referred to as an Apache violin.

There are also fiddle traditions among the Athabascan of Alaska, the Navajo of New Mexico and Arizona, and the Metchif. The Metchif, also called Turtle Mountain fiddlers (after the place where the plains of North Dakota meet the Turtle Mountain), are a mix of Chippewa, Cree, French Canadian, and Scottish. The names and styles of the tunes reflect this grand mixture of cultures. A Metchif fiddler can perform a "rabbit dance" right after a hoedown.

In southern Arizona, the people of the Tohono O'odham (Desert People Nation) play the fiddle as well. The music reflects Native American, Mexican, and European influences, and the repertoire combines the rhythms of schottisches, polkas, two-steps, and mazurkas with the melodies of O'odham ritual dances.

The music of scratchy twin fiddles in Native American culture is fondly referred to in some areas of the United States as "chicken scratch."

Support Materials: Native American

Violin Voices: Traditional Music from the Old Pueblo

This one-hour video features four musicians: a country fiddler, an Apache violinist and violin-maker, a mariachi violinist, and a fiddler in a Tohono O'odham Waila band, each playing his own traditional music from and around Tucson. (Southwest Series)

Medicine Fiddle by Michael Loukinen

In the process of making this film, Loukinen visited several reservations in North Dakota, Wisconsin, northern Michigan, Manitoba, and southern Ontario, where he recorded Native American fiddlers and step dancers. *Medicine Fiddle* shows how Native American fiddling in the northern Midwest is largely performed outdoors, at least in the summer months, and how, historically, it got a foothold in the remote logging camps that employed Native American men. Available on video, the film features several Turtle Island fiddlers and dancers. (Up North Films)

Wood That Sings: Indian Fiddle Music of the Americas

This anthology of Native American fiddle music features performances by Native American musicians from Nova Scotia and Manitoba, to North Dakota and Arizona, to Mexico, Peru, and elsewhere in Latin America. Using this most popular of instruments as a way to explore the great variety and creativity of Native American musical traditions—from chicken scratch to the indigenous Apache fiddle—this recording expresses the capacity of Native cultures to adapt and synthesize non-Native influences. (Smithsonian Folkways)

The Crooked Stovepipe by Craig Mishler

Named for a popular local fiddle tune, *The Crooked Stovepipe* explores the indigenous fiddle music and social dancing of the

Athabaskan people. Craig Mishler taped and interviewed *Gwich'in* fiddlers and dancers, whose territory spans the border between Alaska and Canada along the Yukon River. His book is based on a series of twelve visits, each about a week long, from 1972 to 1992. (University of Illinois Press)

🎵 Discography: Native American

Cherokee (contemporary): Golana, *Feather on the Wind* (Oginali Productions)

Shivwit Paiute (contemporary): Arvel Bird, *Big Chief Quetoos,* (website: www.arvelbird.com)

Shivwit Paiute: *Paiute Country Fiddle* (website: www.arvelbird.com)

Tohono O'odham: The Gu-Achi Fiddlers, *Old Time O'odham Fiddle Music* (Canyon)

Various Tribes: *Borderlands: From Conjunto to Chicken Scratch, Music of the Rio Grande Valley of Texas and Southern Arizona* (Smithsonian Folkways)

Plains Chippewa/Métis: *Turtle Mountain Music* (Folkways)

Chippewa: *Metchif Tunes from the Turtle Mountain* (Burnt Woods)

Scandinavian

When we refer to Scandinavian fiddling (also called Scandi fiddling), we are primarily discussing the fiddle styles of Sweden and Norway. There are active fiddle traditions in Denmark, Finland, and Iceland, but these traditions are less known outside their borders.

The *Hardanger* fiddle (in Norwegian, *hardingfele*) is often called the national instrument of Norway. It is similar to the violin, and each one is a handmade work of art. The Hardanger fiddle is distinguished in part by the additional four or five strings that run underneath the fingerboard. These sympathetic strings add echoing overtones to the sound.

The Hardanger fiddle has been chronicled as dating back as early as 1651. The instrument probably originated in the area around the Hardanger fjord of Norway and can be found in several provinces of Norway today. The "flat fiddle" (European violin), as it is called, is also active in Norwegian music.

Norwegian music, referred to as *"hardingfele* music," includes well over 1,000 distinct tunes, or *slåttar,* for the instrument. Each tune has a history and lineage, transmitted as carefully as the tune itself. Tunes are played for listeners, but especially for dancers.

In Sweden, the fiddle is the symbol of dance music, and every area has its own regional style and repertoire. Sweden is known for the *nyckelharpa*—in effect, a cross between a fiddle and a hurdy-gurdy. The oldest image of the nyckelharpa dates back to 1350. This instrument has been popularized worldwide by the virtuoso Swedish band Vasen. Roughly fifteen versions of the nyckelharpa have been documented, and at least four versions are still played today—an uncommon situation for most folk instruments.

The modern chromatic nyckelharpa has sixteen strings: three melody, one drone, and twelve sympathetic. It has about thirty-seven wooden keys arranged to slide under the strings. Each key has a tangent that reaches up and stops (frets) a string to make a particular note. The player uses a short bow with the right hand and pushes on the keys with the left. The nyckelharpa has a three-octave range (starting with the same low G as a violin's fourth string) and sounds something like a fiddle, only with a wonderfully eerie resonant drone.

Finland was ruled by Sweden from the twelfth to the nineteenth century, and by Russia from 1809 until it finally won its independence in 1917. Finland preserved its rich heritage of folk music by aurally passing music, including Swedish fiddle tunes, down through generations. The small harp-like instrument known as the *kantele* has been the most important instrument in the Finnish tradition. The violin or fiddle came relatively late to Finnish folk music, but it is now an important instrument, along with the accordion.

In general, the rhythmic phrasing for most Scandinavian tunes is quite tricky for violinists from other traditions to learn. It always looks innocent on paper but is never played how it appears. In fact, it would be quite impossible to accurately notate the style—in particular, the three beats of a measure that often divide the time asymmetrically.

In addition, this genre is very expressive, and it is often difficult to determine the difference between the tune and the player. Therefore, it is not clear what to notate, and even a fiddler familiar with the style needs to hear at least three different players' versions of the tune before claiming to "know" it. There are a few rhythmic variations along the time axis that are commonly used as ornamentation: starting a note slightly early, for instance (often with a little pulse on the real beat), or slightly syncopating/dotting some of the sixteenths in a set of four.

A fiddler who plays a dozen tunes well from a particular tradition would have no trouble reading another such tune and playing it stylistically correctly.

Also of particular note is Swedish twin-fiddling. The recent addition (in the 1920s) of the second fiddler, who plays in tight rhythmic unison with the first, mirroring his or her ornamentation while fiddling in harmony, altered this tradition. Swedish fiddling prior to the 1920s was played in unison with one fiddle an octave apart ("grov och grant"), a convention also followed in Norway. Chordal accompaniment was also common. As is the case with old-time fiddle repertoire, some Scandinavian tunes on violin require unconventional tunings: A, D, A, E; A, E, A, E; and A, E, A, C#.

Support Materials: Scandinavian

 Nyckelharpskola, Volumes I and II by Peter Hedlund

This instructional DVD for Swedish nyckelharpa playing is available in Swedish or English. (Leydon Graffix)

🔿 *The Rough Guide to the Music of Scandinavia*

Notes and transcriptions of the music of Sweden, Finland, Norway, and Denmark are presented in CD-ROM format. Old local music traditions are covered, as well as innovative developments. Twenty-three tracks give an overview of many of the important players and groups of this genre. (World Music Network)

📖 *Favorite Swedish Fiddle Tunes* by Tom Gilland

This fiddle book includes all the popular Swedish styles, but without ornamentation. (Mel Bay Publications)

📖 *Swedish Fiddle Music: An Anthology* by Ben Paley

This book presents fifty-three transcribed tunes, most with harmony parts. A companion cassette features thirty-three tunes. Now out of print, this is probably the best tune book and recording of Scandinavian fiddling available, so it is well worth looking for a used copy. (publisher unknown)

🔿 Discography: Scandinavian

Finnish: Arto Järvelä, *Järvelä Plays Fiddle* (Oart)

Finnish: JPP, *String Tease* (NorthSide)

Finnish: *Traditional Music from Finland* (Ocora)

Norwegian: Knut Buen, *Hardanger Fiddle Music of Norway* (Saydisc)

Norwegian: Annbojørg Lien, *Aliens Alive* (North)

Norwegian: Sven Nyhus, Hans Brimi, Knut Hamre, and Annbojørg Lien, *Devil's Tune* (NorthSide)

Swedish: Peter "Puma" Hedlund, *Vägen* (Tongång Records)

Swedish: Nyckelharpa Orchestra, *Byss-Calle* (North)

Swedish: Hjort Anders Olsson, *Hjort Anders Olsson* (Giga)

Swedish: Björn Ståbi and Ole Hjorth, *Folk Fiddling from Sweden* (Nonesuch)

Swedish: *Three Swedish Fiddlers* (Shenachie)

Swedish: Väsen, *Live at the Nordic Roots Festival* (North)

Swedish/American: Andrea Hoag and Loretta Kelley, *Hambo in the Barn* (Azalea City)

Scandi/American: Bruce Sagan and Andrea Hoag, *Spelstundarna* (Sagan and Hoag)

Tango

In the 1880s, a number of circumstances and events transpired in Argentina. First, a heavy stream of immigrants from Europe and Africa found their way to Buenos Aires. Among the several million European immigrants (at least half of whom were Italian, and thirty percent Spanish), men greatly outnumbered women, which created a booming industry for the local red-light district on the outskirts of the city. In addition, the German immigrants brought with them a new instrument: the *bandoneon* (resembling an accordion). At the same time, the Araucanian Indians, who were nomadic *gauchos* (fierce horsemen), were cleared from the plains around the city.

Structural changes in the social and economic organization of Argentina during this time period, in combination with increasing foreign investment and the export of agricultural commodities, inspired the government to clear the gauchos from the plains in order to take advantage of its financial possibilities for Buenos Aires. All of these changes resulted in a tremendous economic boom for the wealthy of the country.

The lower classes of Buenos Aires were forced to live on the outskirts of the city. The intermingling of cultures helped produce the music and dance that became known as *tango*. African rhythms, beat on *candombe* drums (known as tan-go), were mixed with *milonga*, a three-century blend of Araucanian and early Spanish colonial music. The original tango dance form was improvised. This required improvisation on the part of the band as well, which ranged from solo piano to a duo or trio with flute, violin, guitar, and/or bandoneon. The musicians improvised in response to the emotions and gestures portrayed by the dancers.

Salon dances involving a man and a woman embracing were the precedent for tango. The Viennese waltz and the European contradanza had already introduced scandalous body contact between couples. Tango went far beyond the innocent hand-holding or hand-around-the-waist of these dance forms. It depicted a sexual enactment between a woman and her man, between two men fighting over a woman, or between a prostitute and her pimp or john.

Once tango became the rage in Paris, initiating its journey into "proper society" around the world, the art form became highly choreographed—and therefore tamed—and composed. Edited out were the improvisatory character of the music and the dance; the spontaneous interaction between musician and dancer; and even, to a large degree, the earthy sexual nature. In fact, it is said that Astor Piazzolla, heralded today as the most important composer in this genre, received death threats after the debut of his first tango compositions. He had altered the music that much.

Tango music is not bound to a fixed pattern of accents, and there are multiple rhythmic figures carried out simultaneously between the instruments. These include phrases that sometimes anticipate the beat, sometimes enter directly on top of it, and sometimes fall slightly behind it. These rhythmic qualities express an element of surprise and passion. Use of vibrato is often lush, and slide technique allows the player to tease into phrases rather than always starting them punctually.

Support Materials: Tango

📖 *French Tangos for Violin* arranged by Martin Norgaard

This book features fourteen tangos by French composers, arranged for solo violin with piano accompaniment. (Mel Bay Publications)

📖 *Oblivion* by Astor Piazzolla

Sheet music for a tango composed for violin, cello, and piano. (Tonos)

📖 *Tango en La* by Astor Piazzolla

Sheet music for a tango composed for violin and piano. (Tonos)

📖 *Introduccion al Angel* by Astor Piazzolla

Sheet music for a tango composed for violin and piano. (Tonos)

📖 *Tango Ballet* by Astor Piazzolla

Sheet music for a tango arranged for a string quartet. (Tonos)

💿 Discography: Tango

Gaitan, Mariana, with the Pedro Chemes Quartet, *Tangos* (Chemes)

Ma, Yo Yo, *Soul of the Tango: The Music of Astor Piazzolla* (Sony Music)

Paz, Fernando Suarez, with Astor Piazzolla, *Tango Zero Hour* (Wea/Atlantic/Nonesuch)

Piazzolla, Astor, with various artists, *The Soul of Tango: Greatest Hits* (Milan)

Tools In the Classroom and Out   *8*

Music-Minus-One Accompaniments

Learning a new musical style is like learning a new language. The technical components of the genre are important, but without the proper articulation, neither the melody nor the improvisation will sound authentic.

Accompaniments provide stylistically appropriate rhythmic and harmonic grooves that facilitate mastery of new styles. This backup support is essential for students working on improvisatory skills.

We all wish that we could have a live band handy and at our beck and call. However, particularly considering that the only accompaniment available in the past was a metronome, the CDs and software accessible to us today are groundbreaking and a more-than-adequate substitute.

Band-in-a-Box by PG Music is the most popular play-along software today. Made for both PC and Mac, the program requires a computer, a cable, access to speakers or a stereo system, and either an internal music card (such as the Roland Virtual Sound Canvas) or an external sound module (a small piece of hardware that translates the computer's signals into sound). If you find technology intimidating, a local music store (such as Sam Ash) or PG Music will walk you through the steps necessary to set up your system.

Once installed and on screen, Band-in-a-Box is easy to use. Just type in the chords for any song, using standard chord symbols (such as C, Fm7, or C13♭9), choose from a number of available styles (jazz, pop, country, classical, and more), and Band-in-a-Box will do the rest. This consists of automatically generating a complete, professional-quality arrangement of piano, bass, drums, guitar, and strings.

Jamey Aebersold's *Jazz Aides* provides another music-minus-one option, offering over one hundred CDs with accompaniments to blues and jazz standards. There are also accompaniments for all twelve major and minor scales and for harmonic phrases—such as the II-V-I turnaround—that are popular in jazz.

Support Materials: Music-Minus-One

Bluegrass: *Bluegrass Practice Session* (Homespun Tapes)

Blues: *Jammin' the Blues* (Homespun Tapes)

Cello Drones (Navarro River Music)

Jazz: Play-Along CDs: *The New Real Book* (SHER Music)

Jazz: *Jazz Play-Along Series* (Hal Leonard)

Old-Time: *Slow Jam for Old-Time Music* (Homespun Tapes)

Rock 'n' Roll: *Rock and Roll Back-up Session* (Homespun Tapes)

World Music: *Planet Musician* (Hal Leonard)

Notation Software and Alternative String Scores

Although new materials become available to string musicians every day, notated fiddle literature still dominates the available written resources. Today's computer music software programs, such as Finale by Coda Music, make it extremely easy to scan in a fiddle tune;

to transpose the melody into viola, cello, or bass clef in one click of a mouse; and, in another click, to create a harmony part.

StringsCentral.com also provides access to some of the most recent scores in alternative strings, as well as direct contact information for their composers. The site is constantly expanding and has a search engine that organizes data on the basis of skill level, group size, or style.

Alternative String Clinicians

There are a number of talented, experienced alternative string clinicians available to come to schools and work with classes or student orchestras. A complete database is available at StringsCentral.com, comprised of the names, credentials, and geographic availability of many of the major clinicians in the field.

Training Programs, Fiddle Camps, and Internet Sites

There are many wonderful programs available that you can attend—mostly during the summer—to hone your playing and teaching skills in the alternative string arena. These include both fiddle camps (such as Jay Ungar's Ashokan Fiddle Camp, Swannanoa, Augusta, and the Mark O'Connor Fiddle Camp) and accredited programs (Vanderbilt University and American String Teacher, among others). In fact, name any style, and, chances are, a summer program exists that offers training by some of its top proponents.

Internet sites abound that are chock full of information on existing and upcoming string clinics, concerts, books, CDs, discussion groups (such as Fiddle-L and the International Association of Jazz Educators String Caucus), and more.

Please visit the Alternative String Corner at AmadeusPress.com for access to all of the above information.

Inspirational
Role Models

9

There are a few string players who defy categorization and require their own special spot in this book. This is because each one is a unique trailblazer whose life has influenced every individual he or she has had contact with through performances and workshops. Each one has explored many styles and made major contributions to our string community.

Improvising cellist **David Darling**, through his organization Music for People, has introduced thousands of string players and instrumentalists/vocalists throughout the world to creative improvisation. From his work with Paul Winter Consort to his solo recordings on ECM, his music reflects exploration of the deepest nature.

When we look at jazz violin and fiddle history, there are very few female names on the rosters of those who have come before us. Times are different now. Outstanding female fiddlers such as **Natalie MacMaster** and **Eileen Ivers** have earned international recognition and proved that it was sexism, not a lack of skill or artistry, that kept female players of the past out of the public spotlight. For instance, when asked whom he considered his equal, jazz violinist Stuff Smith unhesitatingly said, **"Ginger Smock."** No one had heard of her. Smock was a California jazz violinist who was conspicuously ignored by the press and the record labels. She died in the 1990s in total obscurity, and her artistry is only now beginning to surface through the efforts of jazz historian Anthony Barnett.

Regina Carter was the first woman violinist to break into the male-dominated jazz field. She has helped open doors to future generations of female instrumentalists. Carter never set out to change the industry. She just did what she loves to do, and did it so well that no one could stop her from moving up in the world.

Freestyle fiddler **Darol Anger**, co-founder of the Turtle Island String Quartet, has dipped his bow into every style imaginable and then some. His unique, one-of-a-kind signature sound, prolific imagination, and untiring educational efforts as a clinician have distinguished him as one of the premiere string players and innovators of our time. His creative projects with the Montreaux Band, Barbara Higbie, the Grammy-nominated Fiddlers 4 (Michael Doucet, Bruce Molsky, and Rushad Eggleston), Four Generations (with artists such as Johnny Frigo, Joseph Kennedy, Jr., and Regina Carter), and Natalie MacMaster, to name just a few, have thrilled audiences worldwide for decades.

photo by Randall Wallaxce

Jay Ungar and Molly Mason

In addition to constantly touring and recording with his partner Molly Mason, fiddler **Jay Ungar** has been running his fiddle camp, Ashokan, for roughly two dozen years. Ungar was one of the first grassroots fiddlers to cross over into the big time and show the world that an alternative string player can be a star and even make a good living! He toured with David Bromberg's band back in the 1970s and paid his dues as an area fiddler before his tune, "Ashokan Farewell," was introduced in the late 1980s in the Ken Burns Civil War series on PBS.

Mark O'Connor started performing as a fiddler at an early age. After recording with dozens of well-known country and bluegrass artists in Nashville on hundreds of albums, O'Connor branched out into swing and classical. His work as a composer has teamed him up with classical cellist Yo Yo Ma and, as a jazz artist, with trumpeter Wynton Marsalis. With more than 150 public performances, his "Fiddle Concerto No. 1" has become the most-performed modern violin concerto. Most of the time, classical players try to cross over into alternative fiddle or jazz styles. O'Connor went in the opposite direction: from fiddling to classical and jazz. He has proven that a fiddler can make it into the White House to perform, and that the walls we are taught to believe hold us into one single-minded life effort do not exist where passion and commitment are concerned. His fiddle camp, the Mark O'Connor Fiddle Camp, offers a stellar faculty of guest instructors.

This book is dedicated to **Howard Armstrong** (1909–2003). Part Cherokee, part African American, Armstrong fiddled the blues, string band music, and old-time music for close to a century. He could tell a story like no one else, and, as a member of Martin, Bogan, and Armstrong, he kept the string band tradition alive. He taught me that, while technique provides mobility on the instrument, playing is nothing without the full heart and soul of the player. He imbued every note with a heart big enough to make up for all the folks who haven't discovered their hearts yet. Thanks, Howard.

Howard Armstrong

Where Do We Go from Here?   *10*

We can't expect our mindsets to change instantly. Most of us were taught to follow a certain set of rules, to play what was set down in front of us, and to move from Book One to Book Two—whether of Applebaum's String Builder series or Suzuki. We are accustomed to being spoon-fed. In addition, many of us have emerged from a training system that may have inadvertently negated or subverted our love of music due to the extreme pressure to build technique.

Many string educators have mentioned to me at conferences that when they purchase an alternative string book, they don't know what to do after they have finished presenting the material it offers. Our field is so new that, for most of the styles discussed in this book, sequential educational plans do not yet exist. Rather than waiting for the next publication, approach this as a creative challenge: invent your own next steps. Let go of the old model that made us fearful of proceeding incorrectly or making mistakes, and blaze your own trails. Encourage your students to pursue quality while enjoying the rich treasures music has to offer.

Index

78-RPM, 82

A

AABB, 52–53, 148, 151
aboriginal, 148
Acadian, 68, 147
accent, 32, 53
acclaim, 12
acclimate, 38–39
accompaniment, 35, 39, 46–48, 76–77, 119–120, 142, 152, 156, 164, 171, 174, 177
accordion, 65, 156, 170, 173
accuracy, 36
acoustic, 36, 62, 71, 95, 104, 115–116, 126, 128–129, 142
Acuff, Charlie, 57, 77
Aebersold, Jamey, 99, 109, 147, 178
Afghanistan, 139
African American, 183
African, 13, 22, 46, 56, 139, 141, 173, 183
African *gonje*, 139
Afro-Caribbean, 65
Afro-Celtic, 150
Afro-Cuban, 22, 37, 98, 141–142
agave, 167
age, 1, 26, 33, 55, 61, 66, 91, 100, 131, 136, 150, 162, 182
air, 34, 38, 52
aires, 76, 148, 151, 173
Aladdin Laddies, 71

Alaska, 167, 169
Albert Arsenault, 150
albums, 55, 65, 95–96, 133, 182, 187
algebra, 27
Alphonso Trent Orchestra, 93
alternative, xi, 2–3, 5–6, 14, 16–17, 21–22, 24, 28, 36–37, 44, 97, 115, 178–179, 182–183, 185
American, 1, 6, 11, 34, 49–50, 55, 62, 70, 74, 76, 78–81, 83, 85–87, 107, 146, 151, 165, 167–169, 172–173, 179, 183
American Fiddle Styles, 49, 70, 151
American Folklife Festival, 55
American String Teacher Association (ASTA), xi, 6, 187
American String Teacher Conference, 86
amplification, 76, 82–83, 86, 116, 123, 126–132
Amram, David, 2
Anastasio, Paul, 74, 77, 80, 101, 165
Anger, Darol, 6, 56, 60, 79, 85–86, 92, 98, 100, 102–103, 126, 136, 182
ankle, 160
Apache, 139, 167–168
Appalachian, 56–57, 59

Florido, Jesus, xi, 80, 141, 143
flute, 142, 147, 166, 173
Folk Music Society, 1
folk music, 1–2, 15, 59, 75, 82, 140,
    157, 170
folk revival, 53
Fontenot, Canray, 67
forearm, 88
forms, 10, 47, 52–53, 85, 139, 155,
    160–161, 174
formulaic, 8
fortune, 1
foundation, 12, 46, 135, 142
France, 67, 83, 85, 95–96, 103,
    139, 150, 159
Franco-American, 50, 53, 68–70
freestyle, 6, 16, 182
French, 10, 53, 65, 67–70, 85, 95,
    141, 147–148, 167, 174
French-Canadian, 50, 52, 147
frets, 161, 170
frevo, 146
Friedlander, Erik, 107, 110
Friesen, Eugene, 107, 110
Frigo, Johnny, 182
frog, 60, 90
Fruge, Wade, 66
frustrated, 20
function, 7, 9, 34, 60
functional rhythms, 13
funky, 96, 114, 132

G

Gabriel, Edgar, 136
Galamian, 1
Galicia, 150
Galician Celtic, 150, 153
gamaka, 160
games, 2, 16, 45
gaohu, 145
Gardner, Robert, 6, 80
*Garland Encyclopedia of World
    Music*, 140
gauchos, 173
Gellert, Dan, 57

generations, 3, 15, 17–18, 56, 58,
    62, 83, 96, 99, 132, 150,
    164, 170, 182
genre, 3, 10–11, 18–19, 22, 26, 32–
    34, 48, 59, 61–62, 86–87,
    113, 115–116, 142–143,
    152, 162, 165, 171–172,
    174, 177
geography, 11, 165
Georgia shuffle, 43, 54, 63
Gillespie, Dizzy, 94, 105
Gimble, Johnny 71–73, 77, 79
Glaser, Matt, 6, 43, 64, 80, 85,
    100–101, 103
*Glen Collection of Scottish Dance
    Music, The,* 153
gold rush, 49
Goodman, Benny, 1
Goodman, Jerry, 103, 113
government, 7, 24, 173
grace notes, 43, 76, 145–146, 163
Grappelli, Stephane, 61, 79, 83,
    90, 93–97, 101, 103–105
Greece, 156–157
Greek, 139, 156–157
Greenblatt, Deborah, 108, 111
Greene, Bruce, 57–58, 77
Greene, Richard, xi, 38, 43, 59–60,
    62–63, 77, 113
Grissom, Sean, 109–110
grooves, 22–23, 31–35, 38, 56, 58,
    70, 96, 112, 117, 119, 135–
    136, 177
grov och grant, 171
*Grumbling Old Woman: Tunes for
    New England Con-
    tradancing, The,* 70
guidelines, 22
guitar, 17, 36, 38, 45, 51, 59–60,
    65–66, 69, 74, 76–77, 91,
    98, 104, 108, 113, 116,
    128, 130, 133–135, 146,
    156, 166, 173, 178
gutsy, 87, 90, 114, 132
Gypsy, 93, 139–141, 156–159, 162–
    163
Gypsy Fiddler, The, 158
Gypsy Violin, 158

H

Haigh, Chris 78, 140, 156, 164
Hal Leonard Mariachi Series, 166
Haley, Ed, 53
Hammons, Eddon, 53
hands, 19, 31, 38–39, 53, 87–89
Hankins, Elizabeth, 17
Harbar, Mary Ann, 140, 155, 158
Hardanger, 139, 169–170, 172
hardingfele, 169–170
harmonic, 9, 12–13, 32, 35–36, 39,
    46, 52, 83–84, 94, 99, 114,
    116, 177–178
harmonic motion, 9, 32, 35–36, 46,
    84
harmony, 23, 59–60, 71, 108, 171–
    172, 179
Harris, Don "Sugarcane," 113,
    133–134
Hartford, John, 57, 77–78
Hayes, Clifford, 82
Hayes, Martin, 77, 79, 153–154
Hayes, Nap, 82
head, 7, 86–87
heartbeat, 9, 18, 32, 119
Hébert, Donna, 69–70
Hebrew, 162
hemiola, 43, 63
Henry, William, 1
Hicks, Bobby, 59, 65
hierarchy, 11, 14–15, 18, 30, 37, 45
Higbie, Barbara, 182
Higgs, D.M., 90
*High and Lonesome: The Story of
    Bluegrass Music*, 64
high school, 2, 17, 166
hillbilly, 12, 52, 59–60, 62
Hindustani, 160–161
Hinton, Milt 82
historic overview, 49, 81, 83
history, 3, 7, 11, 14, 18, 24, 101,
    107, 127, 140, 142, 144,
    156, 159, 163, 165, 170,
    181
hoedown, 52, 56, 167
Holcomb, Roscoe, 58
Holland, Jerry, 77, 149

Holley, Joe, 71
Holly, Buddy, 113
Hollywood, 24
holograph, 47
homogenous, 18
Hooker, John Lee, 133
hornpipe, 52–53, 148, 151
horns, 82, 84, 86, 127, 130, 165–
    166
Hot Licks for Bluegrass Fiddle, 64
Hot Tuna, 132
*How to Play Romanian Folk
    Violin*, 155–156
Howes, Christian, 80, 85, 126
Huastecan, 165
Huichol, 165
Huiksi Music, xi, 44, 92, 100–101,
    106, 136
Hungary, 154, 158–159
huqin, 144–145
hysterical, 88, 121

I

Iceland, 169
images, 20, 31
imagination, 3, 7, 11, 45, 182
imagistic, 29
immigrants, 12, 49, 65, 165, 173
implement, 21
improvisation, 3, 6, 14, 16, 22, 37,
    39, 43–48, 61, 71, 74, 84,
    95–98, 100–101, 107–109,
    111, 122, 133, 135–136,
    142, 144, 146, 157–158,
    161, 173, 177, 181
improvising violin, 48, 100, 136
Indian, 21, 44, 46, 106, 160–162,
    168
Indians, 173
indigenous, 147, 165, 168
inept, 44
information, 9–10, 24, 27–29, 43,
    47, 58, 64, 86, 92, 101,
    135–136, 152, 155, 179
inspiration, 13, 50, 58, 99
inspirational, 181
institutionalization, 12

Robertson, Alexander "Eck," 53, 58
Robeson, Paul, 1, 164
rock, xi, 17, 21–22, 24, 31, 38, 46, 60, 62, 76, 92, 96–97, 99–100, 103, 113–117, 121, 123, 133–134, 136–137, 178
rock 'n' roll, 17, 24, 115, 123, 134, 178
rock tours, 114
rock vibrato, 121
Rockin' Out with Blues Fiddle, 92, 101, 136
rocking chair, 31
Roland Virtual Sound Canvas, 177
role models, 15, 26, 181
rolls, 76, 88, 153, 160
Roma, 157
Romania, 154, 158–159
roneat, 145
roots, 10, 13, 76, 133, 149, 151, 172
Rough Guide to the Music of Scandinavia, The, 172
rules, 7, 14, 16, 98, 185
Rumania, 157
rumba, 141
Russia, 154, 159, 170
Russian, 154–156, 162
Ryan's Mammoth Collection of Fiddle Tunes, 78

S

Sabien, Randy, xi, 33, 99–100, 105, 126
sailors, 167
salsa, 136, 141, 143
Salyer, John Morgan, 53
Sam Ash Quiet Violin, 126
samba, 146
Sane, Dan, 90
sangeet, 160
Sarah Lawrence College, 2
sarangi, 161

scales, 7, 9, 11, 13, 21–23, 29, 33, 41–43, 45–48, 60, 85–87, 89, 92, 100–101, 111, 117–118, 121–123, 136, 157–158, 163, 178
Scandinavian, 34, 53, 107, 154, 169, 171–172
Scheinman, Jenny, 98
Schoeffel, Scott 126
school, 1–3, 11, 14, 17, 27, 92, 123, 128, 134, 166
schottische, 53
Scotland, 11, 150, 153
Scots-Irish, 49
Scottish Fire, 153–154
Scottish, 32, 53, 65, 81, 110, 147–154, 167
scroll, 88, 160
Searcy, Deloise 91
second, 16, 33, 46, 50, 60, 82, 88, 128–129, 131, 171
sections, 8–9, 35–36, 46, 52–53, 64, 71, 84, 101, 108, 113, 115, 120, 139, 142, 166
Seeger, Pete, 1
Seidenberg, Danny 107, 112
self-expression, 9
sequence, 27–29, 31, 105
Serbia, 155
set-tunes, 53
Shankar, L. , 79, 161
sheet music, 28, 41, 76, 85, 116–117, 174–175
Shetland Islands, 151, 154
shifts, 13
shuffle stroke, 13, 32, 35, 48, 53–54, 65
signature, 8, 53, 66, 157, 182
Silberman, Daryl, xi
silence, 20
Sims, Henry Son, 81
singing, 19, 21, 29, 66, 90, 115, 146, 167
skills, 14, 22, 25–28, 30, 38–39, 44–45, 63, 109, 111, 117, 119, 121, 177, 179
Skinner, James Scott, 151
Sky, Patrick, 78

Index_

slåttar, 170
slavery, 81
slaves, 11, 81
Slick, Grace, 132
slide techniques, 21, 160
slides, 20, 61, 63, 65, 76, 87, 89–90,
    121, 143, 145, 160, 163
Slovakia, 155, 159
Smith, Hobart, 53
Smith, Stuff, xi, 83, 90, 93–96, 99,
    101–103, 105, 113, 126,
    181
Smithsonian Institute, 55
Smock, Ginger, 181
smyrneika, 157
society, 1, 12, 14, 27, 69, 174
software, 21, 99, 130, 177–178
solfège, 30, 203
solid-body, 116, 126, 128–130
son jaliscience, 166
son montuno, 141
sonatas, 85, 106
songs, 9, 58–59, 61, 70–71, 74, 82,
    98, 110, 117, 119, 132–
    133, 135, 146, 155–157,
    167, 178
soul, xi, 30, 67, 73, 102, 133, 175,
    183
soulful, 13, 45, 55, 87
sound, xi, 8, 14, 16, 18–21, 28, 30,
    35, 58–60, 64, 68, 72, 75,
    83, 86, 88–90, 93–96, 98–
    99, 105, 110, 114, 116–
    117, 121–122, 126, 128–
    129, 131, 134, 137, 147,
    155, 163, 169, 177, 182
South Memphis Jug Band, 90
South, 56–57, 74, 76, 82–84, 90,
    92–93, 95, 105, 113, 145,
    160–162
South, Eddie, 83, 92–93, 95, 105,
    113
Southern, 11, 58, 115, 165, 167–
    169
Southern Old-Time Fiddle Tour,
    58
Southwest, 71, 168

space, 16, 20, 31–33, 102, 104, 109,
    120
Spain, 11, 140–141, 150, 159
Spanish, 106, 140–141, 165, 173
spatial, 29, 33, 131
speed, 13, 20, 39, 78, 87–89, 95,
    108, 121
Spicher, Buddy, 64–65, 71, 74, 79
spiritual, 9, 13–14, 165
Sprout Wings and Fly, 55
square dance, 24
staccato, 20, 32, 90, 148, 151
stamina, 155
Stein, Andy, 98
Stephens, John L. "Bunt," 53
Stepp, William Hamilton, 53
Stevens, Uncle Bunch, 58
stiff, 19, 38, 41
stigma, 47
stimulated, 28
Stokes, Frank, 90
Storyville, 91, 105
straight, 1, 19, 27, 37, 123, 146
strathpey, 53, 151
Strathspey King, 151
strathspey, 151
string bands, 50, 56, 70, 74–75, 82,
    183
String Groove, 136
strings, xi, 5–6, 20, 35, 38–39, 41–
    42, 48, 51–52, 54, 58, 65,
    75, 81, 89, 92, 95, 98, 100–
    102, 105, 107, 113–114,
    116, 121, 123, 126–127,
    131, 135–137, 139–141,
    145, 155–156, 161, 169–
    170, 178–179
StringsCentral.com, 86, 179
structure, 7, 9, 11–13, 22–23, 32,
    39, 43, 46–47, 52–53, 117–
    118, 144, 148, 151, 161
Stuart, Joe, 59
students, 2–3, 8, 10–11, 14, 16–24,
    26–30, 32–39, 41–48, 52,
    63–64, 68, 76, 78, 85–86,
    88–90, 92, 100, 108–109,
    114–115, 117–121, 123–

203

wrist, 160
written, 8, 20, 30, 52, 76, 78, 116,
        136, 140, 163, 166, 178
wrong, 7, 12, 44, 47

X

xote, 146

Y

Yamaha QY drum machine, 123
years, 3, 9, 17, 25, 27–28, 33, 37,
        51, 55, 59, 61, 73, 75–76,
        78, 81, 92, 94, 97, 113–
        115, 119, 132, 142, 144,
        150–151, 153, 158, 167,
        182
Yee, Helen, 47
Yehudit, 126

Z

Zappa, Frank, 133–134
zemer, 162
Zeta, 129–130
Zoom box, 126, 131
Zydeco rock, xi
Zydeco, xi, 68